LEARN WINDSURFING IN A WEEKEND

LEARN WINDSURFING IN A WEEKEND

PHIL JONES

Photography by Philip Gatward

ALFRED A. KNOPF
New York
1992

A DORLING KINDERSLEY BOOK

This edition is a Borzoi Book published 1992 by Alfred A. Knopf, Inc., by arrangement with Dorling Kindersley.

Art Editor Tracy Hambleton
Project Editor Damien Moore
Senior Art Editor Tina Vaughan
Series Editor James Harrison
Managing Editor Sean Moore
Production Controller Deborah Wehner

Library of Congress Cataloging-in-Publication Data

Jones, Phil.
    Learn Windsurfing in a weekend / Phil Jones:
photography, Philip Gatward.
        p. cm.
    Includes index
    ISBN 0-679-41277-8 :
    1. Windsurfing 1. Title
    GV811.63.w56J65 1992
    767.3'3--dc20   91-58625
                                               CIP

Page make-up by Damien Moore
Re-produced by Colourscan, Singapore
Printed and bound in Italy by Arnoldo Mondadori, Verona.

First American ed.

CONTENTS

INTRODUCTION

WINDSURFING IN A WEEKEND may sound to some like an impossible challenge to the super fit. Perhaps surprisingly though, it is technique, rather than physique, that is most important in this popular and exhilarating activity. Being fairly fit is, of course, an advantage, but not a prerequisite. Windsurfing does, however, improve your general fitness enormously; the radiant complexions and well toned bodies of many enthusiasts bear witness to this. It has broad appeal to people of both sexes and of all ages, from seven to seventy. It is truly a sport for all. This, more than anything, explains the incredible increase in the popularity of this colorful sport over the last decade.

Your passport to the world of windsurfing is provided in the pages of this book. This well structured and concise course will give you all the information necessary to make the best possible start in the sport, and points you in the right direction as you inevitably move on to more advanced windsurfing techniques and more demanding sailing conditions. The journey of a thousand miles begins with a single step, and *Learn Windsurfing in a Weekend* will ensure that those crucial first steps are steady and sure – too many people have been discouraged from the sport because they have picked up bad habits in these initial stages. *Learn Windsurfing in a Weekend* will help you to avoid those pitfalls, and will enable you to get the most out of this invigorating sport. All that remains is for me to wish you the best of luck with the course. Above all, have fun!

PHIL JONES

PREPARING FOR THE WEEKEND

Some necessary advice and information to help you get started on the correct footing on your weekend course

THERE IS SURPRISINGLY LITTLE required in the way of preparation for your weekend course. If you are going to a teaching center they will provide nearly all the equipment you need. You will only have to take a bathing suit to wear under your wetsuit, a pair of beach shoes, and a towel! You do not need to be particularly fit to learn to windsurf. In light winds, the power in the **sail** is easy to handle and things will happen reasonably slowly. Windsurfing is very good exercise, helping to tone

Flag

Windsurfing boots

FANNY PACK
Some form of pouch, such as the one above, is an excellent practical investment for a windsurfer.

GET INTO GEAR
Familiarize yourself with some of the many useful – often indispensable – accessories available to windsurfers (see pp.16-17).

Fingerless gloves

Boom clamp

BOARD
Get to know the various parts of the **board** and **rig** (see pp.10-11).

Towing eye

Head gear

muscles without the fear of injury associated with other, more physical, sports. You do not need to be a strong swimmer, but confidence in the water is important. Your wetsuit and **life preserver** will help to keep you afloat and the **board**, which is never far away, will never sink. Background reading is always helpful. Read the information sent to you by your teaching center. Do not, however, try to jump too far ahead. *Words in bold are given further explanation in the glossary (pp.92-93).*

WETSUITS
Staying warm is essential if you intend to enjoy the learning process. Modern wetsuits are efficient, comfortable, and attractive. They not only protect you against the elements, they also help to keep you afloat.

LIFE PRESERVERS
A **life preserver** provides you with added confidence and protection in the early learning stages. It should fit comfortably and not restrict your freedom of movement.

PARTS OF THE BOARD

*Fixtures and fittings on the **board** and **rig***

THE SAILBOARD IS THE SIMPLEST form of sailing craft. Highly maneuverable and extremely portable, this very simplicity provides the added thrill of a closeness to the elements unknown in other forms of sailing. The crux of the design rests on the unique free-pivoting **rig** system, which, supported by the sailor, allows the **board** to be steered without the use of a rudder. Although certain features displayed here will only become relevant as you develop new skills, it is helpful at this stage to familiarize yourself with various parts of the sailboard.

BOARD AND RIG

The sailboard is comprised of two main parts, the **board** and the **rig**. The skin of the board is usually molded from some form of plastic, and is filled with foam for buoyancy. The deck has a non-slip surface and a slot in the center through which the **centerboard**, a large retractable fin, is fitted. A small fin is fitted at the rear end of the board. The rig consists of the **sail**, the **mast**, the **boom**, and the **mast foot**.

BOOM •
Most **booms** now have a **clamp** at the front end to fasten onto the **mast**.

MAST FOOT •
The **universal joint** joins the **rig** and the **board** together. The bottom end of the **mast foot** fits into the **mast track**, running along the **centerline** of the board, which can be used to adjust the rig position.

TOWING EYE •
Many **boards** are fitted with a **towing eye** at the front and/or rear.

BATTENS

Battens slide into pockets on the **sail**. They help to maintain the sail shape. The length and number of battens will vary depending on the size and design of the sail. They are fastened with buckles on the **leech**.

OUTHAUL

The **outhaul** rope is used to attach the **clew** of the **sail** to the end of the **boom**. Pulleys in the **outboard** boom end fitting enable the rope to be tightened without a great deal of fuss.

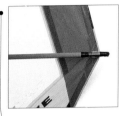

BOOM

The **boom** length is normally adjustable to accommodate the different sizes of **sail**. If the boom is too long, controlling the **rig** is more difficult and power is lost.

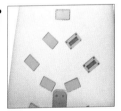

FOOTSTRAPS

Modern **boards** have fittings for **footstraps**. Used only in stronger winds, they are rather a hindrance to the early learning stages, and so should be discarded until they are required.

FIN

A small but vital feature, the **fin** gives the sailboard directional stability.

CARRYING EQUIPMENT

The best way to lift and transport your **board** *and* **rig**

ONE OF THE GREAT ADVANTAGES of windsurfing is that the equipment is extremely portable. Sailboards lend themselves perfectly to roof racking. They are relatively light, and can easily be lifted by the average adult. Although both **board** and **rig** are relatively durable, care must be taken when transporting or carrying equipment. As well as damage to the sailboard, injuries to others are possible. However, problems can be avoided by adhering to a few common sense precautions.

CARRYING BOARDS

This should present no real problem; it is very much a matter of technique rather than physique.

CHIN UP •
Keep your head up and your back straight while lifting.

HANDS •
One hand holds the **universal joint**. If this is not fitted, simply slide your fingers into the **mast track**. The other hand holds the **centerboard**, which extends beneath the **board**.

FOLLOW THE LEADER •
The tapering ends of the **board** are convenient for this method of carrying a board.

PAIRING UP
Small adults and children will find it much easier if they can pair up. Standing at each end allows the arm to extend right around the **board**.

ROOF RACKS

SECURE YOUR GEAR

Two bar, ladder-type racks are the most popular with windsurfers. The rack must be firmly secured, with the bars as far apart as possible. Ensure it is well padded to protect the **board**. Straps of at least 25mm (1 inch) wide should be used to attach the board at each end; and the ends of the **mast** that extend beyond the car should be marked.

CARRYING RIGS

The **rig** can be carried in a variety of different ways. Always keep the **mast** across and into the wind, allowing the rest of the **sail** to fly out behind it. Let the wind do most of the work.

OVER THE TOP

One hand supports the **mast** above the **boom** and the other hand holds the boom itself. This method is ideal when you are carrying the **rig** into the wind.

• WIND LIFT

This is not nearly as difficult as it looks. The wind does most of the work for you by blowing underneath the **sail** and lifting it.

LIFTING •

Again the hands grasp the **mast** and the **boom**, but this time on top of, rather than underneath, the **rig**. Remember to bend the knees, rather than the back, when lifting.

SAFETY FIRST

To avoid damage to the **rig** or, worse still, other people, rigs should always be secured when left ashore.

• BACK

To keep the **mast** across the wind it may be necessary to walk backwards if you are using this method.

WETSUITS

Styles of suits for all seasons

THE MODERN WETSUIT has revolutionized water sports. The efficiency of the new breed of wetsuit makes windsurfing feasible all year round. Apart from the sailboard, the wetsuit will be your single biggest investment. Give careful consideration as to which will be most appropriate for the conditions in which you are likely to sail.

WINTER

In the winter months, suits about 4–6mm (⅛in) thick are normally essential. These wetsuits are usually known as steamers.

NECK SEAL
This helps to keeps out water.

STEAMER
This is a very popular option for the winter sailor. A well fitting steamer is almost watertight, but is still very flexible.

ZIP
Climb into your suit from the back.

KNEES
Most suits are now reinforced. Knees are particularly liable to damage, although patches can be replaced by the wetsuit's manufacturer if necessary.

DRY STEAMER
Probably the warmest suit of all. All the seams are sealed up to prevent water getting in, and the suit is very closely tailored for a good fit. It is known as a steamer for reasons that will very soon become apparent if you wear it.

KEEPING WARM

HOW A WETSUIT WORKS

Wetsuits work in two different ways. The material used to manufacture them has excellent thermal properties and helps to retain body heat. Thus, the thicker the suit, the better the protection offered. Also, they allow a thin layer of water to form between the body and the suit, this heats up and in turn helps maintain body temperature.

DOUBLE LINED

All wetsuits have a nylon lining on the inside and some of them have a lining on both sides. The lining on the inside allows the wetsuit to slide easily over the skin, and the lining on the outside helps to prevent the suit snagging. The lining does tend to retain water which can make the suit slightly less comfortable to use.

SUMMER

During the summer, windsurfers often revert to wearing sleeveless tops and shorts to make the most of the sun.

ARM OPTION •
Steamers often have detachable arms, so that they can also be used in summer.

SHORTY •
Suits without either arms or legs are known as shorties. They are ideal for the summer months.

VEST •
If it gets really hot, vests are available in a great variety of colors.

SNUG •
Wetsuits should fit tightly on the legs, chest, and waist, but looser on the arms.

BRIGHT •
Bright colors have always been popular with surfers. There is no shortage of choice.

BREEZY •
Some people prefer to wear cotton shorts. Remember, though, that wetsuits also protect you from abrasions.

CLOTHING

Essential accessories for windsurfing

THE WETSUIT IS THE windsurfer's main item of personal equipment, but if you are to be comfortable and enjoy the sport in safety there are a number of other accessories to consider. Just what to wear will depend on the climate. In warm weather, the extremities, such as hands and feet, are not likely to suffer from the effects of cold. In the winter months additional protection may be necessary. Whatever the weather, always wear your **life preserver**.

• GLOVES

Gloves must not affect grip. They can protect the hands from blisters and help to keep them warm. Leather sailing mittens offer good protection from abrasions while leaving fingertips free for more delicate work; neoprene (a synthetic rubber) gloves are more restricting but better for keeping out the cold.

Sailing mittens

Neoprene gloves

HEAD PROTECTION •

Between a quarter and a third of all body heat is lost through the head and back of the neck. In winter, the neoprene helmet gives ultimate protection. However, a warm, well-fitting woollen hat, even if wet, will be effective in retaining body heat.

• SHOES

Good grip is essential. Lightweight windsurfing shoes with non-slip soles will give added grip and protect the feet against abrasions from objects under the water.

• BOOTS

In cold weather, neoprene boots will not only aid grip but also keep feet warm. Balance might be affected by cold feet, so boots are a good idea for those sailing in the winter.

HELMET
Polystyrene hats provide maximum protection as well as warmth.

WAIST HARNESS
Once some of the basic techniques have been mastered, a **harness** will conserve energy by transferring the force of the wind away from your arms to the body.

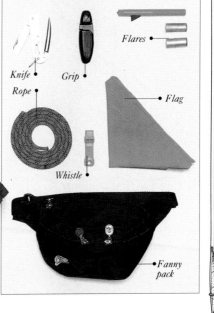

HARNESS LINES
Most **harness lines** are made of rope. Some of them utilize a plastic covering to help prevent wear and tear. They are normally attached to each side of the **boom**, with webbing or buckles, in order to spread the load.

SEAT HARNESS
The seat **harness** has become the most popular for recreational use. The hook is usually below the waist and the force is taken by the bottom rather than the back. The **rig** is supported almost entirely by the weight of the sailor.

LIFE PRESERVER
A wetsuit provides some flotation. However, the **life preserver** gives additional support when in the water, and warmth when out of it.

LIFESAVERS

FLARES
If you do get in trouble, flares and flags can alert others. You may well be able to make minor repairs while still afloat.

Flares

Knife

Grip

Rope

Flag

Whistle

Fanny pack

GONE WITH THE WIND

The power in the sail

THE WIND IS NATURE'S driving force. It is invisible, but its effects
are clear enough, particularly when it blows hard. It is to the
sailboard what gas is to the car, but has the advantage of being free!
Wind-driven vehicles, however, although cleaner, are generally less
reliable than those powered by fossil fuels. The wind can vary in
strength and direction and has enormous power. This is the reason
why even experienced windsurfers treat the elements with a
healthy respect. As a beginner, it is worth picking the right wind
conditions to sail in. If there is too much wind, time afloat will be
frustrating, as you will not be able to handle the conditions. The
force of the wind is usually measured on the Beaufort Scale, which
is based more on the effect of the wind than its actual strength. In
the early stages, try to avoid winds over force 4.

THE DRIVING FORCE
Windsurfing relies on tapping the energy
of the wind and, by use of the **sail**, turning
it into forward motion. The sail acts in
much the same way as an aircraft wing,
generating lift as the air passes over it.

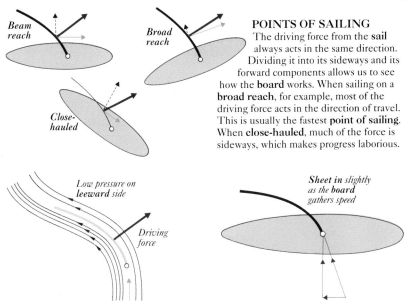

Beam reach

Broad reach

Close-hauled

POINTS OF SAILING

The driving force from the **sail** always acts in the same direction. Dividing it into its sideways and its forward components allows us to see how the **board** works. When sailing on a **broad reach**, for example, most of the driving force acts in the direction of travel. This is usually the fastest **point of sailing**. When **close-hauled**, much of the force is sideways, which makes progress laborious.

Low pressure on leeward side

Driving force

Sheet in slightly as the board gathers speed

SAILS SUCK

The wind on the **leeward** side has to travel faster than that on the **windward** side as it has further to go. The resulting low pressure means that the **sail** is sucked sideways.

AIR APPARENT

As the **board** moves forward, a **head wind** is created by its own forward motion. The effect of this is that, as the board accelerates, the **sail** has to be pulled in slightly.

BEAUFORT SCALE

No.	CRITERION	DESCRIPTION	VELOCITY *(knots)*
0	*Sea like a mirror; smoke rises vertically.*	*Calm*	*less than* 1
1	*Rippling effect on water; smoke drifts.*	*Light air*	1 – 3
2	*Small wavelets; weather vanes move.*	*Light breeze*	4 – 6
3	*Large wavelets form; light flags extend.*	*Gentle breeze*	7 – 10
4	*Whitecaps form; small branches move.*	*Moderate breeze*	11 –16
5	*Whitecaps; some spray; small trees sway.*	*Fresh breeze*	17 – 21
6	*Large waves form; large branches swaying*	*Strong breeze*	22 – 27
7	*Breaking waves; whole trees in motion.*	*Near gale*	28 – 33
8	*High waves; branches snap.*	*Gale*	34 – 40

POINTS OF SAILING

The directions in which the sailboard can travel

IT MAY SEEM difficult to believe as you take your first tentative steps afloat, but, with practice, a sailboard can be sailed in any direction, apart from directly into the wind. Although there is no clear divide between the different courses, they are collectively referred to as the **points of sailing**.

RUNNING •
The **board** is said to **run** when the wind is directly behind it. This is normally the most difficult, and is therefore the last, **point of sailing** covered.

BEAM REACH •
The **beam reach**, where the wind is blowing at about 90 degrees to the side of the **board**, allows you to sail across the wind in one direction and then back in the other, returning to the position from which you set out.

Broad reach

CLOSE-HAULED •
There is an area of approximately 45 degrees on either side of the wind direction into which a **board** cannot possibly be sailed. The **sail** will simply flap like a flag and will not drive the board forward. To sail towards a target directly **upwind**, you must sail on either side of this **no go zone** on a **close reach** or **close-hauled** course, with the sail **sheeted in** over the **centerline** of the board.

Head to wind

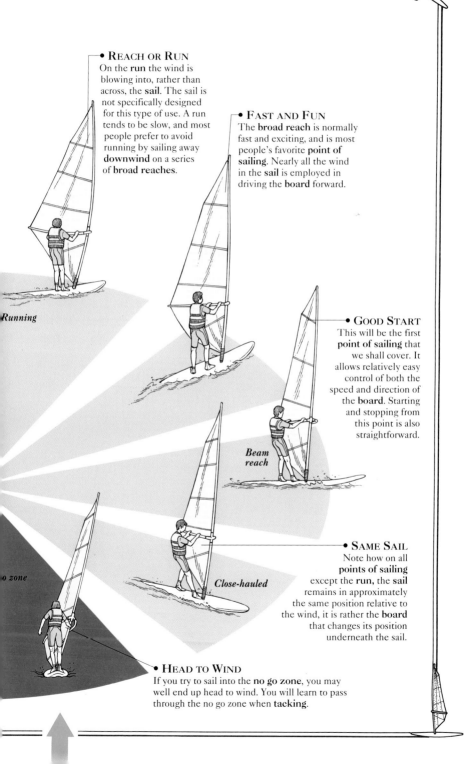

• REACH OR RUN
On the **run** the wind is
blowing into, rather than
across, the **sail**. The sail is
not specifically designed
for this type of use. A run
tends to be slow, and most
people prefer to avoid
running by sailing away
downwind on a series
of **broad reaches**.

• FAST AND FUN
The **broad reach** is normally
fast and exciting, and is most
people's favorite **point of
sailing**. Nearly all the wind
in the **sail** is employed in
driving the **board** forward.

Running

• GOOD START
This will be the first
point of sailing that
we shall cover. It
allows relatively easy
control of both the
speed and direction of
the **board**. Starting
and stopping from
this point is also
straightforward.

*Beam
reach*

Close-hauled

• SAME SAIL
Note how on all
points of sailing
except the **run**, the **sail**
remains in approximately
the same position relative to
the wind, it is rather the **board**
that changes its position
underneath the sail.

o zone

• HEAD TO WIND
If you try to sail into the **no go zone**, you may
well end up head to wind. You will learn to pass
through the no go zone when **tacking**.

THE WEEKEND COURSE

An at-a-glance timetable for your two-day training course

•

THE WEEKEND COURSE is divided into 14 skills. Day 1 covers the **rig** assembly, familiarizes you with the sailboard, and teaches the basic steering principles. This will give you confidence on the water and enable you to guide yourself safely back to the shore. The second day is devoted to the more challenging **points of sailing** and covers self-rescue, which explains how to meet any difficulties that may arise. Choose a weekend when settled weather and light breezes are forecast. It makes sense to start on inland waters, as they have no strong tides or currents. Don't feel obliged to complete the course in a weekend. Take it at your own pace – enjoy yourself!

DAY 1		*Hours*	*Page*
SKILL 1	Rigging	¾	24-27
SKILL 2	Launching	½	30-31
SKILL 3	Secure position	½	32-35
SKILL 4	180 degree turn	½	36-39
SKILL 5	Sailing away	¾	40-45
SKILL 6	Steering	1	46-49
SKILL 7	Stance	1½	50-51
SKILL 8	Returning to shore	½	52-53

Secure position

KEY TO SYMBOLS

CLOCKS

Small clocks appear on the first page of each new skill. They tell you, through the blue section, how long you might spend on that skill and show where the skill fits into your day. They are intended only as guides.

RATING SYSTEM •••••

Each skill is given a rating according to the degree of difficulty. One bullet (•) denotes that the skill is comparatively straightforward, while 5 bullets (•••••) are given to the most challenging skills.

FIGURES

The blue figures in the mini-sequence at the start of each skill illustrate the stages of the particular skill that are detailed in the photographs. The large blue arrow indicates the direction of the wind in both the mini-sequence and in the photographs. In the smaller mini-sequences accompanying each stage of a skill, the blue figure highlights where that stage fits into the sequence. Numerals above the figures display the order of the sequence, giving at-a-glance reference to the entire maneuver.

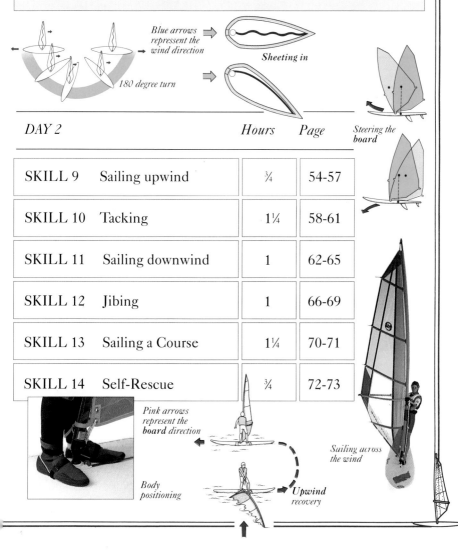

Blue arrows represent the wind direction

Sheeting in

180 degree turn

Steering the board

DAY 2		Hours	Page
SKILL 9	Sailing upwind	¾	54-57
SKILL 10	Tacking	1¼	58-61
SKILL 11	Sailing downwind	1	62-65
SKILL 12	Jibing	1	66-69
SKILL 13	Sailing a Course	1¼	70-71
SKILL 14	Self-Rescue	¾	72-73

Pink arrows represent the **board** direction

Sailing across the wind

Body positioning

Upwind recovery

RIGGING

Definition: *Assembling the* **rig** *in preparation for sailing*

THE **RIG** IS THE ENGINE of the sailboard. Like an engine it must be correctly tuned to produce the best performance. In the early stages, the main difficulties are caused by the use of **sails** that are either the wrong size, or are badly rigged, or even both. A badly rigged sail will lead to all sorts of handling difficulties, which even a very good sailor will have trouble overcoming. Time taken in rigging the sail correctly is always time well spent.

OBJECTIVE: To assemble the **rig** correctly. *Rating* ••••

—————— Step 1 ——————
WHERE TO RIG

If you have a choice it is preferable to rig the **board** on grass, away from other people. Tarmac and concrete will tend to chafe the **sail** and the **boom**, while sand can cause certain parts to stick.

• **BACK TO WIND**
It is surprising how many novices you see getting themselves into all sorts of trouble with their **sail**, simply because they have neglected the first rule of rigging: keep your back to the wind.

LUFF TUBE •
Unroll the **sail**, and then feed the **mast** head carefully up the **luff tube** from the bottom of the sail.

• **FEEDING THE MAST**
Push the **mast** all the way to the top. If the **sail** has an adjustable top, ensure that the tip of the mast is firmly engaged. Tie off the top loosely so that it can be adjusted later.

MAST FOOT ASSEMBLY

1. A **mast foot** assembly comes in several parts.

Mast foot

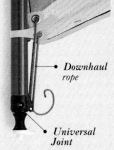

Downhaul rope

Universal Joint

2. The **universal joint** clips into the **mast foot**, which in turn fits into the bottom of the **mast**. Take care not to get grit on the mast foot.

Strap

3. Thread the **downhaul** rope through the eyelets in the **sail** and lightly tighten it. The strap around the **mast**, and the elastic that holds the thick **uphaul** rope, are both secured.

Step 2

BOOM HEIGHT

The next step is to establish where to attach the **boom**. The boom height has a significant effect on stance and must therefore be set correctly.

MARKING THE SPOT
Hold up the **sail** and note the point on the **mast** level with your shoulder. It is helpful to mark this point on the mast permanently with some tape.

WIND
While you are holding up the **mast**, it is helpful to note the wind direction. The **sail** will flap out like a flag. If you are standing facing the sail, the wind will be coming from behind you.

FOOT CARE
Take care to avoid damaging the **mast foot** on hard ground.

SKILL

1

FITTING THE BOOM

The **boom** can now be fitted over the **mast** and **sail**. Check that the boom is the right way up by ensuring that the thick **downhaul** rope lies towards the bottom of the sail.

• BOOM CLAMP
Ensure that the joint between the **mast** and the **boom** is as solid as possible.

• OUTBOARD
Secure the **sail**
the **outboard** en
of the **boom** wit.
the **outhau**
At this poir.
tighten all c
your **batten**

A GOOD FIT
It is important that there is no unnecessary play at the ends of the **boom**, which would make the **rig** difficult to control.

DOWNHAULING

Now the basic controls are attached, they can be tensioned to put shape into the **sail**. **Downhauling** is the next important step.

PUSH AND PULL •
Tighten the **downhaul** by sitting on the ground and pulling the rope, while pushing the **mast** away from you.

BOWLINE KNOT

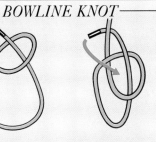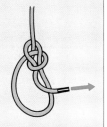

1. To begin with, form the rope into the shape of a loop.

2. Take the end through the loop, pass it around the back.

3. Pass it back down through the hole it came out of.

4. Finally, pull the whole thing tight.

KNOT A PROBLEM
Modern **sails** use **cleats** to fasten the ends of ropes, therefore a knowledge of knots is not a priority. If you own an older model, the bowline knot (see above) is useful.

─── Step 5 ───

OUTHAULING

With modern **sails** the **outhaul** rope requires much less tension than the **downhaul** and can usually be pulled on with one hand. If more tension is required, use the same method as was used for the downhaul.

HANDY HINT
You can purchase special grips to save burns on your hands (see p.25). Wrapping the rope around a piece of wood or your penknife will serve the purpose just as effectively.

LOOSE ENDS
Once all the controls have been set, the loose ends must then be tied off to prevent them coming undone and ensure they do not get tangled. Remember, however, that it may be necessary to undo them quickly in an emergency, particularly the **outhaul**.

• SMOOTH SAIL
There should be no horizontal creases in the **sail** after tensioning.

SKILL

1

Mast head

Batten pocket

Adjustable boom

HOTWAVE

FINE TUNING

Once the **outhaul** and **downhaul** are set, the **boom** and **mast** lengths may need altering. This is the fine tuning stage of the process.

ADJUSTABLE HEAD
Adjust the head so that the **foot** of the **sail** is as close as possible to the **mast foot** when the **downhaul** has been fully tensioned.

BATTEN POCKETS
Check that your **battens** are adequately secure. There should not be any creases visible in the batten pockets.

BOOM LENGTH
Adjust the **boom** so it is not too long, after the **outhaul** is tightened.

SAIL SHAPE

The shape of the **sail** will determine its efficiency, and how manageable it will be. The basic shape comes from the design of the sail and stiffness of the **mast**.

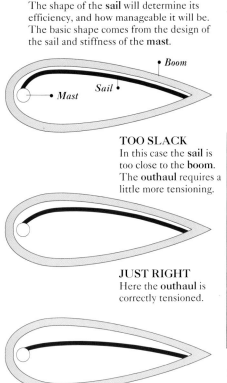

- **Boom**
- **Mast**
- **Sail**

TOO SLACK
In this case the **sail** is too close to the **boom**. The **outhaul** requires a little more tensioning.

JUST RIGHT
Here the **outhaul** is correctly tensioned.

TOO TENSE
Here the **sail** is too far away from the **boom** as the **outhaul** is too tight.

Step 7

CHECK YOUR RIG

The time has come to check that you have put the correct tension into your **sail**. The creases in the sail provide the clues as to any faults that may have arisen from your fine tuning process. Once you are satisfied with the tension the sail is ready for use.

A LAST LOOK
Hold the **rig** upright and check the fullness of the **sail**. If the sail is touching the **boom** then it is insufficiently tensioned and will feel unstable. On the other hand, if the sail has been over-tightened then it will not be able to generate the necessary power.

TENSIONING THE SAIL

HOW MUCH TENSION
The amount of tension required will vary with the design of the specific **sail** and the purpose for which it is being used. The shape of the sail can, however, be altered considerably using the **downhaul** and the **outhaul**. The very full sail, shown in the top diagram, will generate a lot of power but will be heavy and difficult to handle. The very flat sail produces less power and is difficult to handle, with an on or off feel that makes responses unpredictable and awkward. Somewhere between the two extremes is the ideal compromise.

GETTING RID OF CREASES
Modern **sails** should set with relatively few creases. If you find a series of small creases on the **luff** or front of the sail running horizontally, there is more than likely too little **downhaul** tension (see pp.26–27). This will mean making an extra effort, with your foot against the base of the **mast,** to get the extra tension needed. Creases running down the luff normally indicate that there is sufficient tension. Horizontal creases emanating from the **outboard** end of the **boom** suggest too much **outhaul** tension.

2 LAUNCHING

Definition: *Getting your equipment afloat*

WITH THE EQUIPMENT properly rigged, it is now time to take your first steps afloat. There is a great temptation to rush at this stage in your natural eagerness to get onto the water; be warned, however, that time spent familiarizing yourself with the **board** now, will be time saved later. Practice balancing on the board without the **rig**; you will quickly discover that the **centerline** is the most stable area. If you discover the least stable areas, you can test the quality of your wetsuit! Once the rig is added, there is a lot more to think about.

OBJECTIVE: To get the **board** onto the water
and attach the **rig**. *Rating* • • •

Step 1
WHERE TO LAUNCH

Aim to launch into knee-deep water, so you can lower the **centerboard** away from obstructions. Ideally, the wind should blow along the shore so you can sail easily away from land.

TAKE THE PLUNGE
Take the **board** and the **rig** separately to the edge of the water, taking care that the rig is secured, and will not blow away. The board tends to drift away the moment your back is turned, so carry the rig into the water first. Be sure you have fitted the **centerboard**!

Step 2
BOARD AND RIG

Once the **board** and the **rig** are in the water, the two can then be connected by plugging the **mast foot** into the **mast track**. Having the **centerboard** down at this stage aids the process.

TIP THE BOARD
Hold on to the top of the **daggerboard** with your left hand, while supporting the **board** with your legs as shown. Don't attempt this in water that is too shallow or you may damage the fins.

• CONNECTION
Now, simply clip the **universal joint** straight into the **mast track** provided.

ALTERNATIVE LAUNCH

TIME SAVER
As more skills are developed, other much quicker methods of launching can then be adopted. Pick a launching site where the wind is blowing along the shore. Assemble the **board** and **rig** at the water's edge with the front of the board pointing towards the water. When you are ready to go, lift your **mast** with one hand and the back of the board with the other. The wind should blow under the **sail** and the front of the board should just float.

Walk forward into the water, keeping the mast in line with the **centreline** of the board. When in deep water, you can then fully extend the **centerboard** and sail off as normal.

SKILL

3

THE SECURE POSITION

DAY 1

Definition: *The stable position with the* **board** *across the wind and the* **rig** *at right angles to the board*

THE SECURE POSITION is the place to begin sailing from, and, should anything go wrong, it is the place to get back to in order to try again. As the name suggests, it is the easiest and most stable position to adopt. Nearly all the skills in this book start from here, so it is worth spending a little time on.

OBJECTIVE: To raise the **rig** out of the water and adopt and maintain the secure position. *Rating* • • •

Step 1

GETTING ON BOARD

Ideally, you should start in waist-deep water. However, the theory remains the same even if you find you are unable to touch the bottom.

• **LIFE PRESERVER**
The **life preserver** can help at this stage; kick with both legs, as if you are swimming, as you heave yourself onto the **board**.

• **CENTERLINE**
Keep your weight over the **centerline** to avoid tipping the **board**. Bring your legs up and kneel just behind the **mast foot**.

FULL SAIL •
Grasp the thick **uphaul** rope to aid balance. Check the wind direction. It should be blowing from behind you. If not, pull the **rig** up slightly and let the wind blow you around (see p.34).

Step 2
DRAINING THE SAIL

Now stand up on the **board**. Keeping both your arms straight, lean back, and allow the **sail** to drain slowly.

• LIFT THE RIG
Bend your knees slightly and, keeping your head up and arms straight, use the strength of your legs to pull the **rig** slowly out of the water.

Step 3
RAISING THE SAIL

As soon as the **sail** is drained, it can then be pulled all the way up out of the water. Do not be tempted to rush at this stage in the process.

HAND OVER
Work hand over hand up the **uphaul** rope and lift the **rig** out of the water. Maintain the **mast** at ninety degrees to the **board** and resist the urge to reach for the **boom**.

SKILL
3

Step 4

INTO THE WIND

Once the **rig** is out of the water the **board** can be redirected even though the **sail** is not yet full of wind. Small and gentle movements of the rig will enable you to turn the board.

HANDS
From the top of the **uphaul**, transfer your hands onto the **mast**. You may prefer to hold the mast with your front hand only, leaving the other hand free to help you balance.

• TURN
Lean the **rig** towards the back of the **board** and the front will turn to the wind.

FEET •
To maintain balance, your feet should be shoulder-width apart, and positioned over the **centerline**.

UPWIND RECOVERY

TURNING ROUND
There will certainly be occasions when you check the direction of the wind after dropping the **rig** and discover that it is blowing from in front of you when you are facing the **sail**. This makes it much more difficult for you to pull up the rig. In this situation, stand up and lift the rig slightly and allow the sail to drain as you would normally. The wind will catch the sail and blow the **board** gently around. When, eventually, the wind is blowing from behind you, you will be able to pull up the rig, using the **uphaul** in the usual way, and adopt the secure position.

Bring the **mast** *upright*

Gently raise the sail

Step 5
TURN AWAY

You can turn the front of the **board** away from the wind by leaning the **rig** towards the front end of the board.

FOOT STEPS
The **mast track** gives a good guide as to the exact position of the **centerline**, where your feet should be.

STANCE
The feet remain firmly planted over the **centerline** in order to maintain your balance.

SAIL
The **sail** flaps out at ninety degrees to the **board**.

Step 5
SECURE POSITION

Maneuver into the secure position by leaning the **rig** towards the back and the front of the **board**. All your movements at this stage should be small and slow until you are able to anticipate the likely result.

• POSTURE
You should be in a comfortable, relaxed position, with your feet on the **centerline** of the **board**, equally spaced on either side of the **mast foot** around shoulder-width apart. Relax your legs and allow the board to move naturally under you.

SKILL

4 180 DEGREE TURN

Definition: *Turning the **board** through 180 degrees*

NOW YOU HAVE the **sail** out of the water you will be ready to get underway. There is only one more thing to learn before you sail off into the wild blue yonder, and that is how to get back! Remember, also, that there are two ways the **board** can point in the secure position, and you may not be facing in the right direction to sail away from the shore. A basic method of turning the board around is, therefore, essential even at this early stage. Once again, we start from the secure position.

OBJECTIVE: To turn the **board** around. *Rating* ••••

––––––– Step 1 –––––––
SECURE POSITION

We have already seen that a **board** can be turned by leaning the **rig**. The 180 degree turn is an extension of this.

• SAIL
If you are in the correct position at this stage, the **sail** will be flapping out just like a flag, with the wind blowing across both sides. You can maintain this secure position with either both hands, or just the back hand, placed on the **mast**.

LOWER BODY •
Try to relax, but keep your back straight. Your feet should, once again, be positioned over the **centerline** of the **board** to maintain balance. They should be around shoulder-width apart.

BACK TO FRONT
If you get confused as to which is the front and which is the back of the **board**, which can often happen in the heat of the moment, remember that the **mast foot** is always in front of the **centerboard**.

Step 2
INCLINE THE RIG

Initiate the turn by inclining the **rig** towards the back of the **board,** as when you were maneuvering into the secure position. The movement at this stage should be gentle but pronounced.

EASY DOES IT
The speed of the turn is related to both how quickly and how far the **rig** is moved. The faster and greater the movement, the quicker the **board** will turn. Remember, only small, slow movements are required at this stage.

SHOULDERS •
Continue to incline the **rig** in the same direction to keep the **board** turning. Arms remain extended, with shoulders and upper body perpendicular to the rig.

• **RIG**
As you lean the **rig** gently towards the back end of the **board**, the **sail** should then partially fill with wind and the sailboard will be blown forward slightly. The board should begin to feel more stable as a result of this movement.

• **BOOM**
The **outhaul** end of the **boom** can be used as an excellent visual marker for directing the motion of the **rig**.

• **FOOT BATTEN**
The **foot batten** should remain above the surface of the water. If it makes contact then you must be leaning the **rig** too far and are very likely to end up losing your balance and taking a dive.

• **FEET**
Feet remain on the **centerline** in the early part of the turn, and the legs are relaxed with the knees slightly bent.

—————— Step 3 ——————
THROUGH THE WIND

As the turn continues, the front of the **board** turns into, and finally through, the wind. It is your foot position that is the most crucial aspect of the third stage in this particular movement.

RUN THROUGH
Look across the entire set of pictures for this skill sequence. Note how the back of the **board** turns underneath the **sail** as you incline the **rig** and step around the base of the **mast**. Thus you will find yourself back in the secure position with the sailboard facing in the opposite direction from the starting position.

RIG •
Continue to lean the **rig** in the same direction, towards the back end of the **board**, and the front will turn towards the wind. To increase the speed of the turn, move the rig further back.

SAIL •
As the **sail** is not full of wind it will be light and relatively easy to manage.

• **ARMS**
Your arms should remain extended at this stage, with hands gently gripping the **mast** just below the **boom**.

BACK TO THE WIND •
Body weight should be over the **centerline** of the **board**. The wind should be blowing from behind you, with your shoulders remaining more or less perpendicular to the **rig**.

FEET
This is the first time you need to move your feet on the **board**. Take small steps around the **mast**, close to the **mast foot**.

BOARD •
Note how, throughout the turn, the **board** moves underneath the **sail**, but the sail remains in the same place in relation to the wind.

About Face

After every turn, make sure you are back into the secure position before moving on to the next turn or maneuver.

• Posture
You should be in a comfortable, relaxed position with knees and arms just slightly bent. The **sail** will be at ninety degrees to the **centerline** of the **board**.

Step 4
Secure Again

You can now maneuver the sailboard into the new secure position. The front of the **board** will, of course, now be pointing in the opposite direction.

• Face Front
The **board** has turned round; the **rig** is now leaning towards the front of the board.

BACK TO TURN

TURN BACK
The **board** will turn as you tilt the **rig**. To stop the move, the rig must be brought upright. Once you have succeeded in turning the board about, turn it the opposite way.

Empty Sail •

RATE OF TURN
The rate of turn will depend on how far the **rig** is inclined. So the more you lean the rig away from the vertical, and the more quickly you lean it, then the quicker the **board** will turn.

SKILL

5 SAILING AWAY

Definition: *Sailing the board across the wind*

INITIALLY, YOU WILL be sailing across the wind, starting from the secure position. Although we show the skill with the **board** traveling from right to left across these pages, you can, of course, sail in one direction, turn around, and sail back in the other.

OBJECTIVE: To change stance, **sheet in**, sail off and stop. *Rating* ••••

ALL CLEAR
If there are obstructions ahead of you, either wait for them to clear, or turn the **board** around to sail in the opposite direction.

• **POSTURE**
You should be comfortable and relaxed in this position before moving on.

• **FEET**
Maintain the secure position with the **board** at ninety degrees to the wind. Feet should be shoulder-width apart over the **centerline** of the board.

— Step 1 —
SECURE POSITION

Start this skill in the secure position (see pp.32–35). If the **board** is not at the correct angle to the wind, getting underway is more difficult. If things start to go wrong, always return to this position.

GOAL POINT
It is a good idea to establish a goal to sail towards. This will simply help you to check that you are sailing in a straight line, and that you are on a correct course.

• **RIG**
Remember, the **sail** will flap like a flag at ninety degrees to the **board** if it is in the correct position.

MOVING TARGET
Your goal point may be a buoy or post in the water, or something on the shore. Whatever it is, make sure it isn't moving!

Step 2
MOVING BACK

Lean back just a little to counteract the force of the wind against the **mast**, which can make the **sail** feel heavier than it really is.

HANDS •
Let go with the back hand. Your front arm should remain slightly bent. Keep the **rig** at ninety degrees to the **board**.

STEP BACK •
Move your feet back down the board so that the back foot is over the **centerboard** case on the **centerline** of the **board**.

FEET •
Point your front foot forward with your toes next to the **mast foot**.

Step 3
BALANCE POINT

Now, the secret is to draw the **rig** all the way across in front of you until it feels balanced.

• **RIG**
The stronger the wind, the further across the **rig** will need to be drawn.

FACE FRONT •
The **rig** is drawn across by twisting to face the direction in which the **board** will be going. The shoulders and hips should be parallel to the **sail** with the front arm still extended.

BALANCE
At the **balance point** you should be able to release the **rig** momentarily without it falling.

• **WINDOW**
In this position you may be able to see the front of the **board** through the window in the **sail**.

SKILL

5

HAND TO BOOM

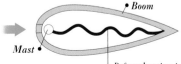

The back hand can now be transferred to the **boom**, as shown, at the point nearest to the back shoulder.

Boom

Mast

Before sheeting in, the empty sail will flap like a flag.

When you sheet in, the sail will blow into a smooth curve. If the sail flaps near the mast, then you have not sheeted in far enough.

BACK HAND
You are able to see where you are heading through the clear window in the **sail**. Note that the back hand is placed lightly on the **boom** at the point nearest to the back shoulder.

BOOM
The position of the **boom** depends on how far the **rig** is pulled across, which in turn relates to the strength of the wind. Hence the importance of the **balance point**.

HANDS
The front hand remains on the **mast**. The back hand rests on the **boom**. There is no need to grip too tight. Remaining as relaxed as possible will help to prevent muscles tiring.

FEET
The front foot, pointing forward, helps to stop you being pulled forward; the back foot, across the **centerline**, resists the sideways pull.

LOWER BODY
The feet stay at right angles to each other. The legs are relaxed and your knees stay slightly bent. Since there is still no wind in the **sail**, maintain your weight over the **centerline**.

COMMITMENT

When windsurfers talk of "going for it", they are usually referring to the mental attitude needed to complete some of the more outrageous stunts possible on a **board**. Huge jumps and even somersaults have been achieved by top windsurfers who are always ready to test the boundaries of their skill. At every level, though, a positive approach is important, and nowhere more so than when getting underway for the first time. Many people tend to fail at this point simply because they are too tentative, and are not prepared to commit enough weight against the **rig** as they **sheet in**. Keep your nerve; although you cannot see it, the wind is there to support you. So go for it, lean back and enjoy the ride. The worst that can happen is a quick ducking.

Step 5

SHEETING IN

The time has come to fill the **sail** with wind. Pull in gently with your back hand. As the sail fills, you will feel the power gradually increase.

MAST
Note how the **mast** now moves upright and that the front of the **board** can be seen beyond the mast.

EASE OFF
Only a small change in the angle of the **sail** to the wind is necessary. If the wind grows too strong, ease out with the back hand to release some of the power.

HEAD
Keep your head up and watch where you are going. Avoid the temptation to look at your hands.

FEET
As the **sail** fills, transfer your weight to the back foot, away from the sail. Keep your front leg straight and your bottom in, so there is a "V" shape between your body and the **mast**.

TWIST
You must twist your shoulders in order to keep them parallel to the **sail**.

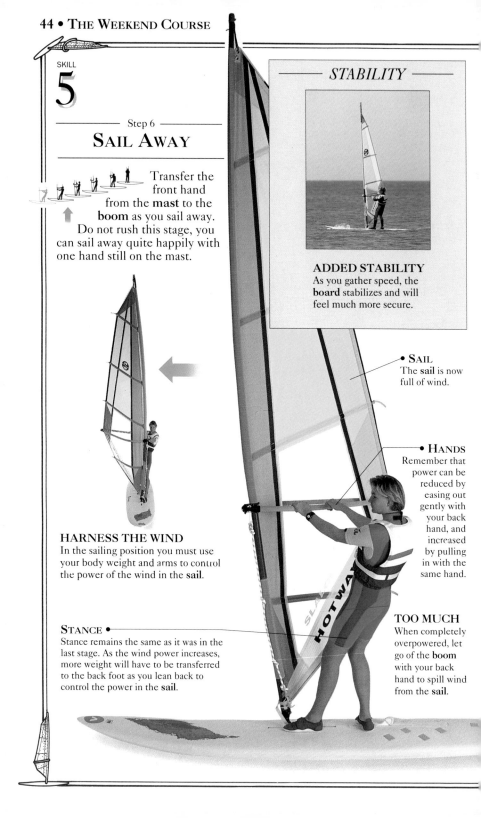

SKILL

5

Step 6
SAIL AWAY

Transfer the front hand from the **mast** to the **boom** as you sail away. Do not rush this stage, you can sail away quite happily with one hand still on the mast.

HARNESS THE WIND
In the sailing position you must use your body weight and arms to control the power of the wind in the **sail**.

STANCE
Stance remains the same as it was in the last stage. As the wind power increases, more weight will have to be transferred to the back foot as you lean back to control the power in the **sail**.

STABILITY

ADDED STABILITY
As you gather speed, the **board** stabilizes and will feel much more secure.

SAIL
The **sail** is now full of wind.

HANDS
Remember that power can be reduced by easing out gently with your back hand, and increased by pulling in with the same hand.

TOO MUCH
When completely overpowered, let go of the **boom** with your back hand to spill wind from the **sail**.

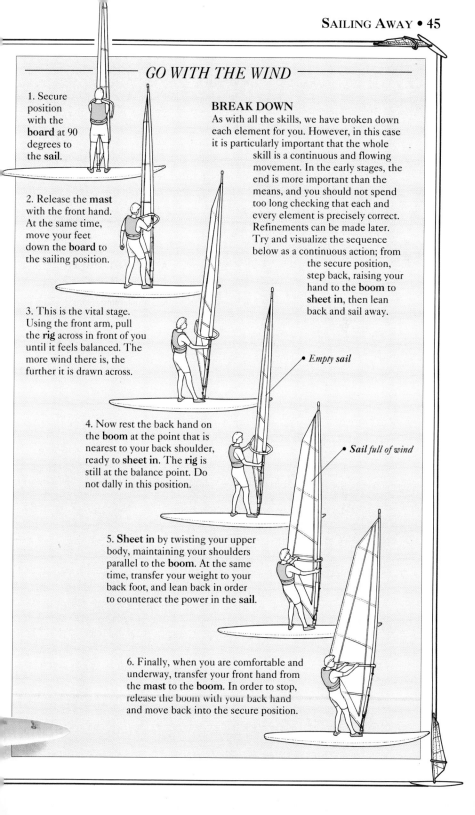

GO WITH THE WIND

1. Secure position with the **board** at 90 degrees to the **sail**.

2. Release the **mast** with the front hand. At the same time, move your feet down the **board** to the sailing position.

3. This is the vital stage. Using the front arm, pull the **rig** across in front of you until it feels balanced. The more wind there is, the further it is drawn across.

4. Now rest the back hand on the **boom** at the point that is nearest to your back shoulder, ready to **sheet in**. The **rig** is still at the balance point. Do not dally in this position.

5. **Sheet in** by twisting your upper body, maintaining your shoulders parallel to the **boom**. At the same time, transfer your weight to your back foot, and lean back in order to counteract the power in the **sail**.

6. Finally, when you are comfortable and underway, transfer your front hand from the **mast** to the **boom**. In order to stop, release the boom with your back hand and move back into the secure position.

BREAK DOWN

As with all the skills, we have broken down each element for you. However, in this case it is particularly important that the whole skill is a continuous and flowing movement. In the early stages, the end is more important than the means, and you should not spend too long checking that each and every element is precisely correct. Refinements can be made later. Try and visualize the sequence below as a continuous action; from the secure position, step back, raising your hand to the **boom** to **sheet in**, then lean back and sail away.

• *Empty sail*

• *Sail full of wind*

SKILL

6

STEERING

Definition: *Making small alterations in course while sailing*

So FAR YOU HAVE only limited control over your destiny when sailing. You are now able to sail backwards and forwards across the wind, stop, and turn around. While this allows you to avoid other people and other things, your course is still rather limited. The next stage is to learn how to make small alterations in course while you are sailing. You will recognize the principles involved.

OBJECTIVE: To change direction by leaning the **rig**. *Rating* •••

Step 1

SETTING OFF

Begin from the secure position; choose a goal across the wind, and set off towards it in the sailing position.

NEW GOAL
From the initial sailing position, look for a new goal slightly further **upwind** than the one directly across the wind.

STANCE
The shoulders are parallel to the **boom** and the arms slightly bent. See how the hands are almost directly above the feet (see p.47).

KNEES •
The knees are slightly bent as you sail away.

AIM
Aim to alter course by no more than 20 degrees at this stage.

PLAIN SAILING

BOOM
In the sailing position, the **boom** will be roughly parallel to the water.

BEARING AWAY
Lean the **rig** forward and to **windward**, keeping it in the same plane.

LUFFING UP
Drop the **boom** towards the water, drawing the **rig** across the body.

Step 2
INTO THE WIND

Turn to the wind. This is done by leaning the **rig** to the back of the **board**.

MAST
The **mast** leans towards the back of the **board**. However, it must not fall away from your body.

BACK HAND
Extend the back arm. Be careful not to pull in too far with your back hand or else you will lose power from the **sail**.

ARMS
Bend the front arm, keeping the **boom** close to your chest.

SAIL
Lean gently to avoid too rapid a response.

FEET
Maintain your foot position. Most weight is on the back foot.

WIND
The aim is to keep the wind blowing across the **sail** throughout the change in course. The sail actually stays at the same angle to the wind while the **board** changes direction under it.

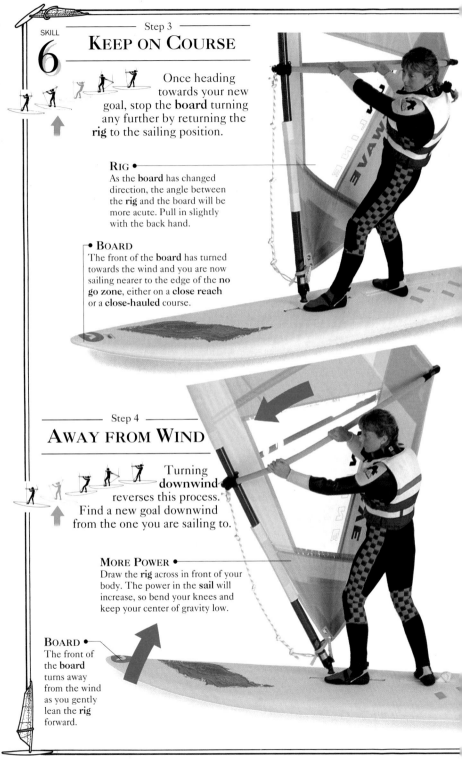

Step 3
KEEP ON COURSE

Once heading towards your new goal, stop the **board** turning any further by returning the **rig** to the sailing position.

RIG
As the **board** has changed direction, the angle between the **rig** and the board will be more acute. Pull in slightly with the back hand.

BOARD
The front of the **board** has turned towards the wind and you are now sailing nearer to the edge of the **no go zone**, either on a **close reach** or a **close-hauled** course.

Step 4
AWAY FROM WIND

Turning **downwind** reverses this process. Find a new goal downwind from the one you are sailing to.

MORE POWER
Draw the **rig** across in front of your body. The power in the **sail** will increase, so bend your knees and keep your center of gravity low.

BOARD
The front of the **board** turns away from the wind as you gently lean the **rig** forward.

Step 5

STRAIGHTEN UP

After having established your new course, you must stop the **board** turning by **trimming** the **rig**.

RIG •
The **rig** is brought back into the upright position with the **boom**, once more, roughly parallel to the water.

STANCE •
The stance alters little as you change direction. It is rather a question of shifting your weight from the front to the back leg.

• **BACK**
Once again, fall back against the pull of the wind in the **sail**.

EASE OUT
As the **board** has turned **downwind**, you can now ease out with the back hand to keep the **sail** at the correct angle.

ARMS
The front arm is extended and the back arm pulls the **boom** close to the chest.

— HOW IT WORKS —

FORWARD
Wind power is focused in the **center of effort**. When this is in front of the **pivot point**, the **board** revolves away from the wind direction.

Center of effort •

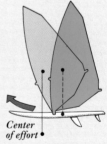

BACK
In a similar fashion, the front of the **board** turns away from the wind as you lean the **rig** backwards behind the **pivot point**.

Pivot point •

STANCE

Definition: *Body posture while sailing*

GOOD STANCE IS VITAL to your enjoyment and progress. It is important, therefore, to develop a good, comfortable, relaxed stance as soon as possible. You can survive in the early learning stages with a few imperfections, but these are bound to hinder you as you try to perfect new skills. Good stance will allow you to handle the power in the **sail** more easily, sail faster in any given wind strength, handle stronger winds more easily, and learn new skills more quickly.

OBJECTIVE: To adopt the most efficient stance. *Rating* •••

POSTURE

The basic stance remains the same on all points of sailing from **close-hauled** to **broad reach**.

• HEAD
Look over your front shoulder to your goal point. This helps avoid the hunched stance, and possible collisions, if you watch your feet.

• SHOULDERS
The shoulders remain parallel to the **boom**, with the arms slightly bent.

• LOWER BODY
The back should be kept straight, the bottom tucked in, and the hips forward. Leave room between you and the **rig** to allow you to respond to wind variations.

• LEGS
The knees and ankles should be flexed to allow the **board** to move freely.

PARALLEL FORCES

The shoulders and hips should always be parallel to the **boom** so that you are pulling in the opposite direction to the force generated by the **sail**.

TRIM SAIL •
The **sail** should be **trimmed** so that it is always full of wind. If the front of the sail starts to flap, you should then **sheet in** slightly.

• **SHOULDERS**
In order to change the angle of the **sail** to the wind, twist your shoulders and bend your arms.

ARMS •
The arms should be just slightly bent, with the hands around shoulder-width apart, equally spaced on the **boom**, either side of the **center of effort**.

HANDY HINTS

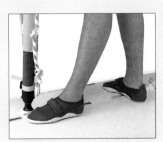

FEET
Feet are shoulder-width apart; the front foot pointing forward while the back crosses the **centerline**.

HANDS
Use your hands like hooks, rather than like clamps, to avoid tiring your arms. Relax your fingers.

8 RETURNING TO SHORE

Definition: *Getting your board back to land*

HAVING IMPRESSED EVERYONE on shore with your skill on the **board**, the last thing you want to do is fall off in the shallows, and surface covered in weed! Too often, coming ashore is simply an unplanned swoop to the nearest landfall, with scant regard to the consequences. Just a little thought at this stage will ensure that the landing is as good as the take off and that you wind up on *terra firma* with the minimum of effort and embarrassment. Over these pages you will find two alternative landing methods. Each has its own advantages.

OBJECTIVE: To head back to shore, drop the **sail**, dismount, and carry the sailboard back onto land. *Rating* • •

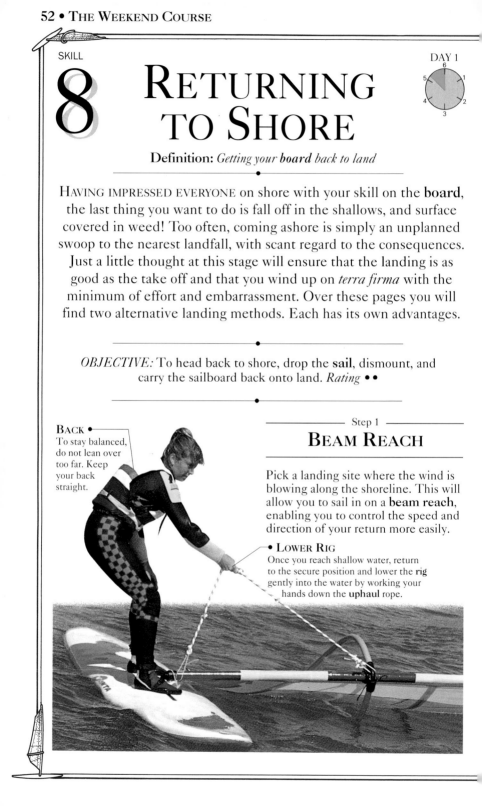

BACK •
To stay balanced, do not lean over too far. Keep your back straight.

——— Step 1 ———
BEAM REACH

Pick a landing site where the wind is blowing along the shoreline. This will allow you to sail in on a **beam reach**, enabling you to control the speed and direction of your return more easily.

• LOWER RIG
Once you reach shallow water, return to the secure position and lower the **rig** gently into the water by working your hands down the **uphaul** rope.

STEP OFF
Drop down onto the **board**, still keeping your weight over the **centerline**. Step carefully off the **board**.

---- Step 2 ----
DETACH THE RIG

Detach the **rig** from the **board** and carry both out of the water. Take the board first as it will drift away. Always carry the rig with the **mast** across and into the wind.

HANDS
Place your hands either side of the **mastfoot**, over the **centerline**, to keep balance.

RIG
Detach the **rig** and let it float until you return after leaving the **board** onshore.

ALTERNATIVE LANDING

BACK OUT
With a little practice the **board** and **rig** can be brought ashore as one unit. Once you have stopped, arrange things so that the front of the board is pointing away from the shore and the rig is on the **downwind** side of the board. Lift the rig by holding the **mast** just above the **boom** and allowing the **sail** to fly. Then lift the back of the board and walk slowly backwards out of the water.

CRASH LANDING
If you are not sure of the contour of the bottom of the stretch of water, be sure to make your approach slowly. If the **centerboard** grounds at speed, you may be dispatched unceremoniously over the front of the **board** as *it* stops and *you* fail to. The centerboard and **fin** are both particularly vulnerable to damage while you are returning to shore.

SKILL

9 HEAD UPWIND

Definition: *Sailing into the wind*

SO FAR WE HAVE SEEN that we can sail backwards and forwards across the wind, and make small alterations in course. This, however, is merely part of the picture. Suppose that our objective is directly **upwind** of our starting point. We know that it is impossible for the **board** to sail directly into the wind. Instead, we must make progress towards our chosen goal by sailing first on one side of the **no go zone** and then on the other.

OBJECTIVE: To progress towards an **upwind** objective *Rating* • • • • •

INITIAL GOAL
From the secure position, choose a goal directly ahead of you and sail across the wind on a **beam reach**.

POSTURE •
Lean back slightly to counter the force of the wind in the **sail**. Keep your back straight and your eyes ahead.

Step 1
ULTIMATE GOAL

First, choose an objective to sail towards **upwind**. As you are in the secure position, this will be behind you.

• **HANDS**
Remember not to grip the **boom** too tightly as this will only serve to tire your muscles out more quickly. If you are too tense, your movements are likely to be stiff and awkward.

• **STANCE**
Keep your front foot pointing forward alongside the **mast foot**. Your weight is slightly biased towards the back foot which is placed over the **centerline**.

Step 2

ALTER COURSE

Now change
your course by
leaning the **rig**
to the back of
the **board**, drawing it
across your body. This
turns the board to the wind.
The change in course should
only be slight at this stage.

RIG •
Incline the **rig** toward the rear of the
board so that the back of the **boom**
almost touches the water. Bend the
front arm to keep the boom close to
your chest and extend the back arm.

• EYES
The **board** will
turn beneath you,
so keep your eyes
on your goal until
the board faces in
the direction that
you wish to travel.

• SAIL
Keep the power
in the **sail** as you
adjust the angle
of your **rig**. The
back hand is
pulled in to allow
you to sail close
to the edge of
the **no go zone**.

SHEET IN
To stop the **board**
turning, return
the **rig** to its
sailing position,
sheeting in
slightly with the
back hand so you
keep the **sail** at
the correct angle.

• BOARD
If the **board** starts to slow
down you may be trying to
sail too close to the wind.
Lean the **rig** forward slightly
and ease in with the back hand
in order to turn the front of the
board away from the wind.

Step 3

BACK UP

Once
you are
facing
in the right
way, bring the **rig**
back upright again
and then resume your
standard sailing position.

• SAIL
If the front of the **sail** starts
flapping, you may need to
sheet in more. If the outer
end of the **boom** is over the
back of the **board** and the
sail still flaps, you are sailing
too close to the **no go zone**.

SKILL
9

Step 4
UPWIND

Although you are now on an **upwind** course, you must turn and sail on the other side of the **no go zone** to reach your ultimate objective.

SHEET OUT
Return to the secure position, and turn the sailboard around through the wind by leaning the **rig** towards the back of the **board**. The momentum will increase stability and help the board to turn.

• FEET
Keep your body in line with the **mast**, taking small steps with your feet close to the **mast foot**. Remember that the further you incline the **rig**, the quicker the **board** will turn beneath you.

BOARD •
The front of the **board** will turn through the **no go zone** until you reach your new secure position on the opposite **tack**.

Step 5
SECURE POSITION

When you resume the secure position on the opposite **tack** your goal will be ahead and to **windward**.

TAKE A BREAK
You are not working against the clock; take as much time as you need in the secure position to gather your forces before setting off again.

FULL TURN •
The front of the **board** is now facing in the opposite direction from the original starting position.

UPPER BODY •
Your back is straight; your hands should now be placed on the **mast** rather than the **boom**. Stay relaxed.

LOWER BODY •
Your feet are placed about shoulder-width apart on either side of the **mast**. Your knees are bent slightly, with your weight over the **centerline**.

Step 6
BEAM REACH

Sail in the opposite direction on a **beam reach**. You will still not be heading towards your final objective at this stage.

NO GO ZONE
If your goal is still **windward** and you cannot reach it without sailing into the **no go zone**, simply repeat the process.

LEGS
Keep your back foot over the **centerline**.

Step 7
ON COURSE

Now you must aim to sail back along the **no go zone** on the opposite **tack**.

KEEP OUT

NO GO
In the early stages do not try and sail right on the edge of the **no go zone**. Keep up your speed.

BODY
Once again you must adopt the standard sailing posture; but this time your left foot is leading, and your left hand is placed forward on the **boom**.

SKILL

10 TACKING

DAY 2

Definition: *Sailing the board through the no go zone*

RETURNING TO THE SECURE POSITION every time you wish to turn, though initially advisable, will quickly become tedious, particularly when sailing **upwind**. The **tack** is a method of sailing the **board** through the turn. As the **sail** is full of wind most of the time and the board is moving, it is much more stable. It makes crossing from one side of the sail to the other safer and less time consuming.

OBJECTIVE: To develop the 180 degree turn. *Rating* •••••

Step 1

CLOSE REACH

Begin by sailing the **board** on a **close reach** near to the edge of the **no go zone**.

TIME TO TACK
Learning to **tack** well means time on the water. Do not expect to be able to do it quickly at first. Once mastered, however, this skill represents a great step in your progression.

SAIL •
Remember that the **boom** must be **sheeted in** near to the **centerline** on a **close reach** to keep the **sail** full of wind.

• **SHEET IN**
The **sail** must be **sheeted in** close to the **centerline** in order to maintain power. If the front edge flaps, sheet in slightly.

• **POSTURE**
For the sake of dignity as well as balance, keep your back as straight as possible while sailing.

• **FEET**
Keep your front foot close to the **mast foot**.

HOTWAVE
SLALOM

Step 2
TURN TO WINDWARD

To initiate the turn, lean the **rig** down towards the back end of the **board**, **sheeting in** slightly to keep the **sail** full of wind and maintain your momentum. The board will then turn towards the wind.

ARMS •
The back arm is extended and the front arm bent, as the **rig** is drawn across the body. Keep looking ahead!

FEET •
The weight is transferred to the back foot, which pushes down on the **leeward** side of the **board**, helping the turn.

Step 3
NO GO SITUATION

As you continue to lean the **rig**, the **board** will turn in towards the wind, and, eventually, inside the **no go zone**. When this happens the **sail** will lose power and feel much lighter.

TIMING
The key to good **tacking** is good timing; knowing the best moment to step around the **sail**.

• **BOOM**
The back of the **boom** will be almost over the **centerline** of the **board** as you try to maintain the power in the **sail**.

KNEES •
Bend your knees a little, keeping your weight low and over the **centerline** of the **board**.

FOOTWORK
Move your front foot so it is placed just in front of the **mast foot** pointing across the **board**.

SKILL

10

Step 4
QUICK STEP

This step has to be quick and fluid. Once the **board** turns through the wind, place your back hand onto the **mast** and then step smartly around the front of the **sail** to the other side of the **board**.

• FORWARD SWEEP
Control the **rig** with the new front hand, sweeping it forward so you continue the turn away from the wind. You may find it easier to have your back hand free to help you balance.

• INSECURE POSITION
Keep your weight over the **centerline** and the **board** flat. With the **sail** and the board in line and nothing driving the board ahead, you are vulnerable to duckings as the board wobbles under you. With practice, however, you will reduce this period of instability.

Step 5
TURNING POINT

By continuing to lean the **rig** towards the front of the **board** you will turn away from the wind. In the early stages, turn until you are sailing on the new **beam reach** course.

STANCE •
Place your feet into the sailing position before finding the new balance point.

INSECURE TACKING

Lean the rig towards the front of the board.

IN THE BALANCE

Until now we have always returned to the secure position, with the **sail** at right angles to the **centerline** of the **board**. There are occasions when it is helpful to start a maneuver without returning to this position every time. **Tacking** is one of these occasions. It is perfectly feasible to set off on a **close reach**. The same rules apply, but you must ensure that the **rig** is at the **balance point** and that you keep your weight low when you **sheet in**. You will discover that you make much better progress like this.

Step 6

SAILING OFF

You can now sail off on a **beam reach** in the normal sailing position. From this easier **point of sailing** you can steer **close-hauled** and repeat the process if necessary.

POSTURE •
Once you have **sheeted in** and harnessed some power in your **sail**, lean back against the pull and resume your standard sailing pose.

THINK POSITIVE
The **tack** does call for a certain degree of commitment. Do not hang around with the **sail** empty for any longer than is absolutely necessary or you will surely fall.

FEET •
Check that your feet are positioned back over the **centerline** of the **board**.

• BOARD
The front of the **board** is once again pointing in a direction heading across the wind. By now you ought to have confidence in your ability to sail away comfortably on this course.

11 SAILING DOWNWIND

Definition: *Sailing away from the wind*

NOVICES MAY BE FORGIVEN for thinking that this is the easiest direction in which to sail. However, your **sail** is designed to have wind blowing across it – not directly into it. As there is no sideways force in the sail to balance against, sailing **downwind** requires you to adopt a different stance.

OBJECTIVE: To sail your **board** on a **downwind** course. *Rating* ••••

Step 1

BEAM REACH

Start off by sailing on a **beam reach** across the wind. But before trying the new skill, check your stance is good.

GOOD START
It is advisable to set off on a **beam reach** simply in order to give yourself more time to visualize your intended maneuver from this relatively easy **point of sailing**.

• **HIPS**
As a gust strikes, drop your hips away from the **rig** to counteract the increased power in the **sail**. As the gust passes, bend your legs and bring your weight back over the **centerline**. Gusts can be dealt with almost entirely by use of the hips!

Step 2
TURN AWAY

The front end of the **board** is turned away from the wind by leaning the **rig** forward.

• RIG
Initiate the turn by drawing the **rig** across and to **windward**. Bend the knees to keep the weight low and avoid being pulled off balance.

EASE OUT
Rather than return to the sailing position, continue the turn by keeping the **rig** forwards and to **windward**, easing out with your back hand.

Step 4
POWER CUT

As the sailboard continues to turn **downwind**, the power in the **sail** reduces dramatically.

HAND SHIFT •
You might find you need to shuffle your hands down the **boom** slightly, towards the outer end, in order to maintain the turn.

• WEIGHT
As the power in the **sail** reduces keep your weight over the **centerline** of the **board**.

• STANCE
Reposition your feet, moving the front foot back to meet the back foot. Pointing the toes slightly outwards will help to control the **board**. Keep one foot on either side of the **centerline**.

SKILL

11

Step 4

RUNNING

The **board** will
continue to turn
until the wind is
directly behind.
You are now heading on a **run**.

• SAIL
The **sail** has now been
drawn across so that it is
at right angles to the **board**.

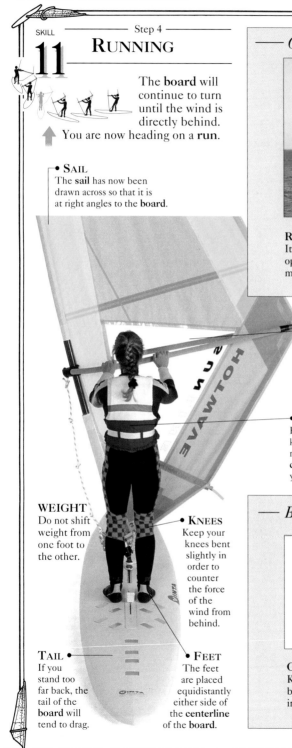

WEIGHT
Do not shift
weight from
one foot to
the other.

• KNEES
Keep your
knees bent
slightly in
order to
counter
the force
of the
wind from
behind.

TAIL •
If you
stand too
far back, the
tail of the
board will
tend to drag.

• FEET
The feet
are placed
equidistantly
either side of
the **centerline**
of the **board**.

— OPPOSITE TACK —

RUNNING BACK
It is possible to **run** on the
opposite **tack** by starting the
move on the opposite **reach**.

• WINDOW
You should now be able to
see where you are going by
looking through the clear
window positioned in the
lower half of the **sail**.

• POSTURE
Keep your back straight, and your
knees slightly bent. Your
weight remains firmly planted over the
centerline. With the wind behind
you there is no sideways force.

— BIRD'S EYE VIEW —

GUSTS
Keep a healthy distance
between you and the **sail**
in order to respond to gusts.

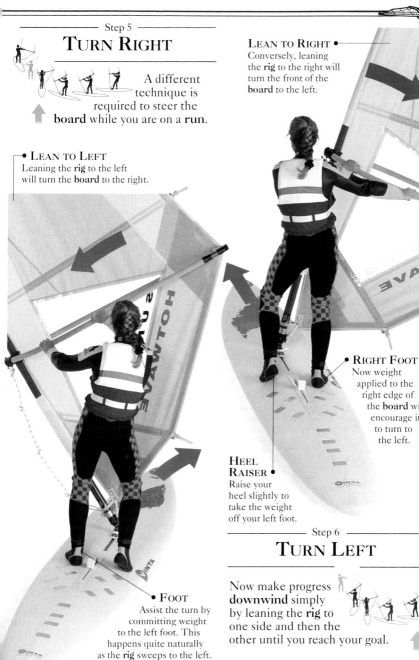

Step 5
TURN RIGHT

A different technique is required to steer the **board** while you are on a **run**.

• LEAN TO LEFT
Leaning the **rig** to the left will turn the **board** to the right.

LEAN TO RIGHT •
Conversely, leaning the **rig** to the right will turn the front of the **board** to the left.

• RIGHT FOOT
Now weight applied to the right edge of the **board** will encourage it to turn to the left.

HEEL RAISER •
Raise your heel slightly to take the weight off your left foot.

• FOOT
Assist the turn by committing weight to the left foot. This happens quite naturally as the **rig** sweeps to the left.

Step 6
TURN LEFT

Now make progress **downwind** simply by leaning the **rig** to one side and then the other until you reach your goal.

ALTERNATIVE
Running is not popular with windsurfers as it is rather slow and ungainly. As an effective alternative to make progress **downwind** you can try **jibing**, which is the next skill.

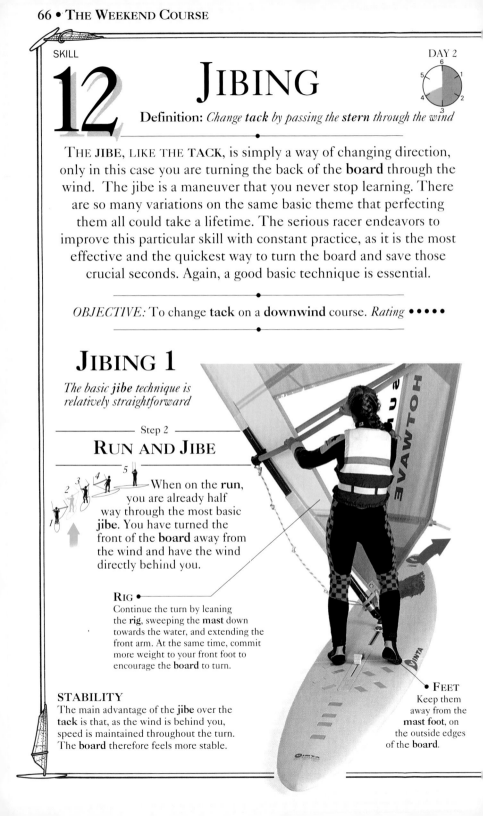

12 JIBING

DAY 2

Definition: *Change* **tack** *by passing the* **stern** *through the wind*

THE **JIBE**, LIKE THE **TACK**, is simply a way of changing direction, only in this case you are turning the back of the **board** through the wind. The jibe is a maneuver that you never stop learning. There are so many variations on the same basic theme that perfecting them all could take a lifetime. The serious racer endeavors to improve this particular skill with constant practice, as it is the most effective and the quickest way to turn the board and save those crucial seconds. Again, a good basic technique is essential.

OBJECTIVE: To change **tack** on a **downwind** course. *Rating* • • • • •

JIBING 1

The basic **jibe** *technique is relatively straightforward*

Step 2
RUN AND JIBE

When on the **run**, you are already half way through the most basic **jibe**. You have turned the front of the **board** away from the wind and have the wind directly behind you.

RIG •
Continue the turn by leaning the **rig**, sweeping the **mast** down towards the water, and extending the front arm. At the same time, commit more weight to your front foot to encourage the **board** to turn.

STABILITY
The main advantage of the **jibe** over the **tack** is that, as the wind is behind you, speed is maintained throughout the turn. The **board** therefore feels more stable.

• **FEET**
Keep them away from the **mast foot**, on the outside edges of the **board**.

Step 3
OVER THE BOW

When **tacking**, the end of the **boom** crosses over the back of the **board**. Now it is flipped so that it passes across the front of the board. The wind swings the **sail** around very quickly.

SAIL
Continue the movement of the **rig**, now sweeping the **sail** towards the back of the **board**.

• BOOM
Release your back hand from the **boom** and pass it under the front arm and so on to the **mast**. As the **rig** swings over, release the boom with your front hand.

• FEET
Twist your feet round, keeping your weight on what was the front foot to help maintain the turn.

Step 4
STOP THE TURN

The front of the **board** will now turn quite quickly into the wind. Bring the **mast** upright to stop the turn and then adopt the secure position on a new **tack**.

RIG
To stop the turn, bring the **rig** back to a central position, controlling it with the new front hand.

• CENTERLINE
Move the feet over the **centerline** and return to the basic secure stance (see p.35).

TWO SIDES
This maneuver can be performed in the opposite direction. Most people find it easier to go one way than the other. The weaker side is the one to practice most!

JIBING 2

With a little practice you will be able to jibe from reach to reach.

Step 2

BEARING AWAY

From the basic sailing position, **bear away** by leaning the **rig** towards the front. Extend the front arm and then **sheet in** slightly so that you turn **downwind**.

MAKING PROGRESS

We are now looking for a quicker and more fluid transition than was possible with the basic jibe. Aim to sail off on a new **tack** without returning to the secure position!

STANCE •
Lean in as you **bear away**. **Sheet out** again as the front of the **board** turns further **downwind**.

Step 3

FANCY FOOTWORK

Keeping the **sail** full, turn **downwind**, moving the feet as if on a **run**. Accelerate the turn by scooping the **mast** down towards the water.

MORE LIFT •
The further the feet move back down the **board**, the more the front will lift and the quicker it will turn.

WEIGHT WATCHING

Moving the feet back may feel uncomfortable at first, but very soon you will be able to get to a short distance from the back of the **board** and it will turn almost on its own axis.

• **FEET**
Push on the right foot to help the turn.

Step 4
MAINTAIN THE TURN

Lean into the turn to
avoid being thrown off.
Keep the upper body
upright, bending the
knees to shift weight.

FLIPPING THE RIG •
The **board** will turn quickly towards the
new **broad reach** course. Flip the **rig**,
releasing the back hand and placing it on
the **mast**. Aim for a smooth transition, with
the **sail** empty no longer than necessary.

STANCE •
Keep more weight over the
leeward edge of the **board**
to assist the turn at this stage.
Keep your legs bent, ready to
step back into the sailing stance.

Step 5
SHEET IN

The back hand is placed on
the **boom** and you can **sheet
in** straight away and sail off.

• **HAND**
To stop the
turn, bring the
mast upright.
Catch the **boom**
in your new
back hand as
it swings over
the **bow** of
the **board**.

FLATTEN THE BOARD •
The feet move forward, ready
to sail away. The foot action
helps to stop the front of the
board turning into the wind.

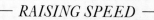
RAISING SPEED

PIVOT
Note how the front of the
board lifts as you commit
your weight to the back.
This helps you turn quickly.

13

SAILING A COURSE

Definition: *Combining the various skills you have acquired*

WELL DONE! You have now learned all the basics. You can sail your **board** on all **points of sailing**, and can **tack** and **jibe**. It is now simply a question of consolidating all you have learned and practicing to develop your embryo skills, to enable you to put them all together in a fluid manner. Perhaps the best way to do this is to sail a course which demands that you apply those new-found skills in a constructive and enjoyable way. Most courses will do this, but the triangle, with one leg set into the wind, is the ideal.

• **JIBE**
The **jibe** is not easy, so do not attempt to jibe too close to the buoy at this stage.

— VISUALIZATION —

In windsurfing, the best route from one point to the other is not always a straight line. It is quite impossible, for example, to sail directly into the wind. It helps if you attempt to visualize each maneuver before you try it, judging the distance required and the direction in which you will travel afterwards. This will help you select the right spot in which to **tack** or **jibe** when you sail around a marker. If in doubt, return to the secure position to consider your next move. In the early stages, passing on the correct side of the markers is success enough. As your **board** control improves, aim to tighten the turns so that you pass close to the buoys. The speed and fluidity with which you perform maneuvers will naturally increase with practice. Likewise, you will become sensitive to the small alterations in your stance that effect board speed. Above all, do not rush!

WINDY ROUTE •
You may be sailing on a **broad reach** or a **run**. Remember that a run is in many ways more difficult and a good deal slower, but it is worth your while to practice running on the occasional circuit, even if only for the sake of increasing your windsurfing repertoire. Experiment by altering course so as to find the quickest **point of sailing**. Try sailing on a broad reach, **jibing** some distance from the buoy.

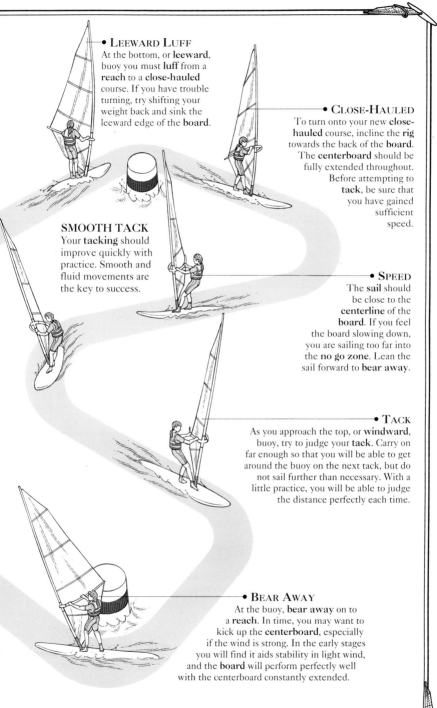

• LEEWARD LUFF
At the bottom, or **leeward**, buoy you must **luff** from a **reach** to a **close-hauled** course. If you have trouble turning, try shifting your weight back and sink the leeward edge of the **board**.

• CLOSE-HAULED
To turn onto your new **close-hauled** course, incline the **rig** towards the back of the **board**. The **centerboard** should be fully extended throughout. Before attempting to **tack**, be sure that you have gained sufficient speed.

SMOOTH TACK
Your **tacking** should improve quickly with practice. Smooth and fluid movements are the key to success.

• SPEED
The **sail** should be close to the **centerline** of the **board**. If you feel the board slowing down, you are sailing too far into the **no go zone**. Lean the sail forward to **bear away**.

• TACK
As you approach the top, or **windward**, buoy, try to judge your **tack**. Carry on far enough so that you will be able to get around the buoy on the next tack, but do not sail further than necessary. With a little practice, you will be able to judge the distance perfectly each time.

• BEAR AWAY
At the buoy, **bear away** on to a **reach**. In time, you may want to kick up the **centerboard**, especially if the wind is strong. In the early stages you will find it aids stability in light wind, and the **board** will perform perfectly well with the centerboard constantly extended.

SKILL

14 SELF-RESCUE

DAY 2

Definition: *Self-help procedure if in difficulties*

YOU WILL NOW be gaining confidence in your ability and be able to avoid conditions that you will have difficulty coping with. Before you get too ambitious, though, it is worth practicing a technique that allows you to get yourself and your equipment back to the shore should anything break, or the wind suddenly die or increase. Remember, always stay with your **board** – you will be more conspicuous, and more buoyant.

OBJECTIVE: To dismantle your **rig** and paddle ashore. *Rating* ● ● ●

SINK OR SWIM?
Do neither. Always stay with your **board**, whether you wait for help or paddle to shore.

WAVE
Raise and lower your outstretched arms above your head.

─── Step 1 ───
IF IN DOUBT

If you find yourself in trouble, you must assess the situation quickly. Attempt self-rescue only if you are reasonably confident of success. If not, you must attract attention to your predicament.

FLARE OR FLAG
Fire a smoke flare, and use your distress flag if you have one. You should!

Step 2
RELEASE THE RIG

If you are a good distance away from land, and the wind grows strong, or the water becomes rougher, folding your **rig** is probably the best option for self-rescuing.

STRADDLE
Sit astride your **board** and leave the **centerboard** down. This will give you a stable platform to work from.

DRIFTING •
If you sit on your sailboard and drift, you will end up in a position with the **rig upwind** of the **board**. This will *not* hinder your progress when you are self-rescuing.

SAFETY LEASH
Unfasten the **safety leash** and remove the **mast foot** from the **board**. Keep hold of the **rig** or it will quickly drift away from you.

Step 3
REMOVE BATTENS

The next step is to remove all of the **battens** so that the **sail** can be rolled up tightly. This is best done before any of the controls are released. Do not rush!

FOOT FIRST
Start at the **sail** foot; remove any **battens** below the **boom**.

MAST SLEEVE •
The **battens** can usually be stored up the **mast** sleeve or **luff tube**. Either push them in from the bottom, or at the **boom** cut out.

• **UNDO THE OUTHAUL**
Once all the **battens** have been removed, unfasten the **outhaul** so that the **outboard** end of the **boom** is free. If you have a rope **inhaul** system, the end of the boom can be thrown towards the top of the **sail**.

SKILL

14

SECURE THE BOOM

If you have a **clamp boom** system, utilize the thick **uphaul** rope to tie the **inboard** end of the boom onto the **mast**.

BOOM
You can now unfasten the **clamp** which holds the **boom** to the **mast** and swing the boom towards the top of the mast. If any of the clamp parts can come off, take care that you do not lose them.

TIGHT ROLL
Pack the **sail** tightly, as shown. The **foot** of the sail will point forward as you paddle. There is a chance of water collecting in the sail and unrolling it if it is not rolled tightly enough.

FOOT FIRST •
Roll the **sail** around the **foot**, working your way carefully towards the **mast**.

ROLL THE SAIL

Now you can roll up the **sail**. Make sure that the sail is rolled tightly, or else it will come undone as you are paddling. Remain calm and take your time with this to avoid difficulties later on.

Step 6
TYING UP

Tie the **sail**, using spare rope, so it cannot come undone as you paddle.

• RIG
Once it is secure, the **rig** is swung underneath you with the **mast foot** pointing forward.

OUTHAUL •
The **outhaul**, which is attached to the end of the **boom**, can be wrapped around the **sail** and fastened off in the **cleat**. This is all that should be required.

Step 7
HEAD FOR HOME

You must now either lie down or kneel on the **board**, and paddle back towards the land.

PADDLE •
Most people are more comfortable lying down and can make quicker progress this way. Use long, deep strokes, as you would if you were swimming the crawl.

• TIP
Do not let the **mast** tip drag behind.

ALTERNATIVES

SOFT OPTION
In light winds, the **board** can simply be paddled with the **rig**, still assembled, balanced across the back of the board.

BOOM BELT
This technique is gaining favor among the experts: remove the **mast foot** and lie inside the **boom** while paddling.

AFTER THE WEEKEND

The next steps to improving your technique

THE NATURE OF PRACTICE is important in these early stages. Now that you have finished your weekend course, choose conditions that will challenge you, but are not beyond your ability. If you cannot cope with the conditions, your time afloat is worthless and you will quickly become disillusioned. Do not only practice the things you can do, but also try to develop new skills. Go with a friend, it is a lot more fun. You may think about joining a club where you can sail and socialize with others of a like mind. Other club members are a valuable source of information.

Choosing a Club

Some training centers have clubs attached to them, and others are run on a voluntary basis by their members. Take time to choose a club; they vary greatly in what they have to offer.

Competitive Windsurfing

As your skills improve you may wish to start pitting your wits against other people. Competition, at whatever level, is the quickest way to improve. Many clubs organize racing, so take this into account when making your choice. For the more ambitious, there is a very strong national racing scene to progress to.

Simply Sailing

However, for most of us, the great attraction of windsurfing still lies in the freedom that it offers and the ever-present challenge of mastering new techniques. It is for this reason more than any other that every weekend, all over the world, people can be seen enjoying the freedom and challenge that is windsurfing.

SAILING ON THE SEA

Ways of tackling waves and tides

WHEN YOU HAVE GAINED MORE confidence you may wish to expose yourself to the challenges of sailing on the sea. Sea sailing is quite different, especially in strong winds, where there is the added challenge from the high waves that can form. Choose conditions carefully for your early outings and treat the sea with a healthy respect. Always choose a venue where others are sailing. This not only indicates that the area is relatively safe, but also means that there will be people who can help should you get into difficulties. Remember, though, that inland waters will usually offer the best conditions for you to develop your basic skills.

WAVE BOARD
Special wave **boards** have been designed for those who enjoy sailing on the sea (see pp.90–91). Very maneuverable and fast, they are only suitable for the more experienced.

SHOREBREAK
Often, the biggest problem created by waves is actually getting away from the beach. At high tide, waves often "dump" on to the beach, making the launching process very difficult. When the tide goes out, the shallow shelving areas of sand near the water are flatter and make launching your sailboard a relatively easy task. Low tide, however, presents the problem of the long walk to the water.

TIME AND TIDE

Tides are caused by the gravitational pull of the Moon, and, less dramatically, the Sun. Tides do not only rise and fall, they also flow back and forth along the coast. Pay particular attention to the direction and strength of the tidal flow.

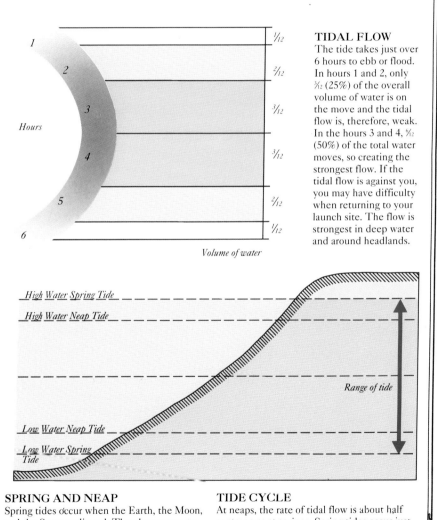

Hours

1

2

3

4

5

6

$\frac{1}{12}$

$\frac{2}{12}$

$\frac{3}{12}$

$\frac{3}{12}$

$\frac{2}{12}$

$\frac{1}{12}$

Volume of water

TIDAL FLOW
The tide takes just over 6 hours to ebb or flood. In hours 1 and 2, only $\frac{1}{12}$ (25%) of the overall volume of water is on the move and the tidal flow is, therefore, weak. In the hours 3 and 4, $\frac{6}{12}$ (50%) of the total water moves, so creating the strongest flow. If the tidal flow is against you, you may have difficulty when returning to your launch site. The flow is strongest in deep water and around headlands.

High Water Spring Tide

High Water Neap Tide

Low Water Neap Tide

Low Water Spring Tide

Range of tide

SPRING AND NEAP
Spring tides occur when the Earth, the Moon, and the Sun are aligned. They have a greater range and come higher up and go further out than neap tides, which occur when the Earth, Moon, and Sun are at right angles.

TIDE CYCLE
At neaps, the rate of tidal flow is about half as strong as at springs. Spring tides occur just after the full and new Moon so there is just over a fortnight between consecutive spring tides. Between them neap tides occur.

WHERE TO SAIL

Choosing the right location in relation to prevailing wind conditions

EVEN WHEN WIND CONDITIONS are excellent, your enjoyment can be marred by choosing the wrong place to sail. In any given wind direction, some places will offer better sailing conditions than others. Try to pick a spot where the wind is blowing **cross** or cross/**onshore**. This will make launching and landing easier and

HEADING FOR TROUBLE •
The wind off headlands is often strong, and the sea can be rougher.

SAFETY IN NUMBERS
The presence of many other windsurfers seems an obvious indication of a good location. Remember, however, to take account of the quality of their performance – they may well be experts enjoying conditions for which you are not yet prepared.

CROSS WINDS
It is easier to launch and land when the wind is blowing in a direction parallel to the beach.

HELP AT HAND
If you can sail with a group, then you have the obvious advantage of help being to hand should you find that you are in difficulties. (see pp.72–75)

FAR OUT •
Before venturing too far out of the bay, where the waves will be bigger, be confident that you can turn around without difficulty.

HEADLANDS
The sea is much rougher here.

• ONSHORE WINDS
Here the wind is blowing directly **onshore**. The waves make launching more difficult.

you will be able to get back to the shore if you should get into any difficulties. Never sail in **off-shore** winds. These can be deceptive as the water looks calm near the beach, but the waves and the wind build up as you get further out. **Onshore** winds are relatively safe, but launching can be difficult. Waves, built up by the wind, dump onto the beach and sailing on a **close-hauled** course heading away from the shore is difficult.

MAN-MADE
Man-made lakes are ideal for novices.

• **INLAND**
As when you were on the coast, launch inland where the wind blows across the shore. A walk round the lake with your kit may save time in the end.

WIND BREAKERS •
Trees and buildings provide effective wind breaks and the wind to **leeward** will be very disturbed. Try to avoid these areas.

WAVES
Even small shorebreakers can hinder the launching process.

Wind direction

WHEN TO SAIL

The best times, conditions, and circumstances for sailing

CHOOSING THE TIME is as important as choosing the place. Your decision will be based on a number of factors, including your competence, the strength of the wind, the state of the tide and, of course, your other commitments.

The Wind

In very general terms, the wind in the summer months tends to strengthen throughout the day, particularly on the coast, reaching a peak at around 3 o'clock in the afternoon. Weather patterns often alter the basic rule of thumb, so you should obtain a forecast to help in your decision. If you have the whole day, try to ascertain when conditions are most likely to be suited to your ability. Remember in the early stages to avoid conditions that are beyond your ability. You will not only become frustrated as you struggle with the **rig**, but you could get yourself into difficulties.

The Tide

If you are sailing on the coast, you will also need to consider the state of the tide. If the tide is high, you will have only a short walk to the water, but the waves may make launching difficult. At many locations waves tend to dump flotsam on to the beach at high tide. If the tide is low, these problems are reduced. Remember, though, that the tide can go out quite a long way at some locations, and the walk can be more exhausting than the sailing.

Your Health

The most important element in the whole equation is you. If you feel at all unwell, you should should not go out. Avoid sailing after a heavy meal, and remember that alcohol affects your balance even when you are on dry land!

SEVEN COMMON SENSES

Handy tips for a safer trip

BEFORE GOING AFLOAT, a moment's thought will
ensure that you get the most out of your sport as
safely as possible. The most basic sailing rules
fall conveniently into seven points referred to
collectively as the "seven common senses":

• **Is your equipment seaworthy?**
All your equipment must be in good condition. Pay
particular attention to ropes and the **mast foot** fitting.
Always replace anything that is showing signs of wear.

• **Tell someone where you are going and when you will return.**
Don't forget to say you are back! Lifeguards have better things to do than look for windsurfers who are comfortably seated in the bar.

• **Obtain forecasts for the local area.**
Check the tide times and think about the tidal effect where you will be sailing. If in doubt, don't go out!

• **Are you capable of sailing in the prevailing conditions?**
Use a **sail** you can handle. Be honest when assessing your own abilities. If in doubt, don't go out!

• **Sail with a friend.**
If either of you should get into difficulties, help will be at hand. Don't try to help if it will endanger yourself.

• **Avoid strong tides, offshore winds, and poor visibility.**
Steer clear of such conditions. With **offshore** winds the sea often appears deceptively calm close to the shore.

• **Consider other water-users.**
Many people make their living out of the sea and must be treated with respect.

RULES OF THE ROAD

Windsurfing etiquette, and essential safety guidelines

THOUSANDS OF PEOPLE use the water for work or pleasure every day. You are not alone, and should always remember that others have as much right to be there as you do. All craft are governed by the International Regulations for the Prevention of Collisions at Sea (IRPCS). These form the equivalent of a worldwide highway code for use on the water. The fundamental rules, which apply to all craft and not just sailboards, are outlined on the opposite page. A good general rule is to try, as far as possible, to keep out of everybody's way, whether on land, as you **rig** your sailboard, or at sea, where you must be constantly alert for other craft and swimmers.

RIGHT OF WAY

There is an old adage that "power gives way to sail", but you would perhaps be pushing your luck if you expected a tanker to give way to a sailboard. The rule applies only when two vessels of a similar size converge. Remember that despite the fact that it does not have a rudder, the sailboard is still possibly the most maneuverable craft on the water. Sailing is a pleasure activity, and confrontation is best avoided.

BASIC RULES

There are three basic rules, outlined on this page, that cover most of the situations likely to arise should two sailboards meet. Accidents may occur if a windsurfer is unaware of who is responsible for taking avoiding action.

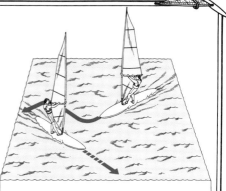

ON OPPOSITE TACKS
On opposing **tacks** a sailboard with the wind on its **port** side must always give way to the one with the wind to **starboard**.

ON THE SAME TACK
The **board** to **windward** must give way to the board to **leeward**. If you are leeward, and someone sails close by you to windward, they will, literally, take the wind out of your sails.

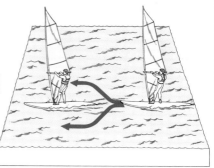

OVERTAKING
If you intend to overtake another sailboard, you must remember to keep your distance!

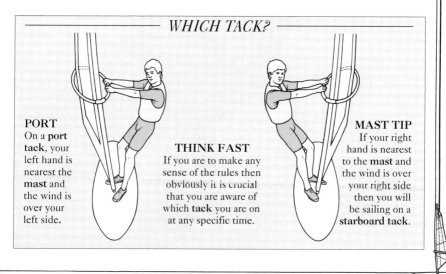

WHICH TACK?

PORT
On a **port** tack, your left hand is nearest the **mast** and the wind is over your left side.

THINK FAST
If you are to make any sense of the rules then obviously it is crucial that you are aware of which **tack** you are on at any specific time.

MAST TIP
If your right hand is nearest to the **mast** and the wind is over your right side then you will be sailing on a **starboard tack**.

STRONG WINDS

How to cope with, and enjoy, sailing in windy conditions.

COMMITMENT AND GOOD TECHNIQUE are the keys to sailing in stronger winds. Everything happens much more quickly, and you must be ready to use all your body weight to control the increased power in the **sail**. This means committing your whole weight to the **rig** which can lead to the odd ducking as you master the technique. Windsurfing in strong winds can be a truly exhilarating experience.

STANCE

From the secure position you must draw the **rig** further across, to bring it to the **balance point** in stronger wind.

SHEET IN
Keep your arms straight. Make sure your hands are positioned correctly before you **sheet in**.

HANG ON
Commit weight to the **rig** as the power comes on, by falling backwards against the **sail**. The **mast** should stay as upright as possible.

FEET
Before **sheeting in**, move your feet further back down the **board** in anticipation of the extra power in the **sail**.

BEAT THE GUSTS

ARMS
Arms should stay straight to ease the forearms and distance you from the **rig**.

FEET
The **windward** edge lifts with the force. The front foot counteracts this.

HEAD
Look ahead to anticipate gusts that appear as dark patches on the water.

GO WITH THE WIND
You should no longer **sheet out** and allow gusts to pass. Aim to use the power to accelerate, stay **sheeted in** and move ballast in and out as necessary.

• **BEND**
Bend at the waist and straighten the legs as a gust strikes.

FAR OUT
Note the space between your body and the **sail** as you lean against the wind.

UPRIGHT STANCE
Smaller variations in the strength of the wind can be compensated for by simply straightening your body and standing more upright.

HIP ACTION
The hips do the work by moving your center of gravity as a gust hits.

STANCE
Keep the **rig** upright in the fore and aft plane, leave the maximum area exposed to wind for full power.

• **AFTER THE BLAST**
If the wind dies significantly, thrust your hips towards the **sail**. Bend your knees and arms, and come up under the **boom**, bringing your weight back over the center.

BUYING A BOARD

*Varieties of **board** and **sails** available.*

THERE ARE MANY SAILBOARDS on the market. Factors such as where and how often you will be sailing, your size, and, of course, the size of your bank balance, will help to narrow down your options.

ALL- AROUND FUNBOARD
These **boards** are 3.4–3.75m (11–12¼ft) long, 180–225 liters volume. Their volume makes them an excellent first time bet.

MID-LENGTH
At 3–3.4m (9½ft) long, 180–225 liters, it makes a good **board** to progress to and is ideal for a child.

BOARDS

The more volume a **board** has, the more weight it will support and the better its performance in light winds.

SLALOM
At 3m (9½ft) or less, about 130 liters, it needs wind of force 4 plus.

CUSTOM BOARDS
These are built to suit the requirements of the individual sailor. The designs vary depending on whether they are used for slalom, speed, or wave sailing.

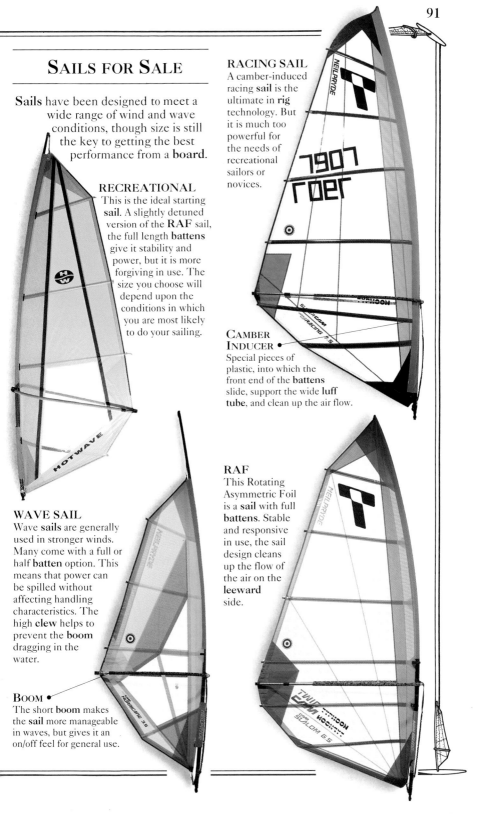

SAILS FOR SALE

Sails have been designed to meet a wide range of wind and wave conditions, though size is still the key to getting the best performance from a **board**.

RECREATIONAL

This is the ideal starting **sail**. A slightly detuned version of the **RAF** sail, the full length **battens** give it stability and power, but it is more forgiving in use. The size you choose will depend upon the conditions in which you are most likely to do your sailing.

RACING SAIL

A camber-induced racing **sail** is the ultimate in **rig** technology. But it is much too powerful for the needs of recreational sailors or novices.

CAMBER INDUCER •

Special pieces of plastic, into which the front end of the **battens** slide, support the wide **luff tube**, and clean up the air flow.

WAVE SAIL

Wave **sails** are generally used in stronger winds. Many come with a full or half **batten** option. This means that power can be spilled without affecting handling characteristics. The high **clew** helps to prevent the **boom** dragging in the water.

BOOM •

The short **boom** makes the **sail** more manageable in waves, but gives it an on/off feel for general use.

RAF

This Rotating Asymmetric Foil is a **sail** with full **battens**. Stable and responsive in use, the sail design cleans up the flow of the air on the **leeward** side.

GLOSSARY

Words in *italic* are glossary entries.

A

• **Apparent wind** The apparent direction of the wind as a combination of the actual wind direction and the motion of the sailboard.

B

• **Balance point** The position to which the *rig* is drawn before sailing away. The rig feels weightless at this point.
• **Battens** Stiffeners which run across the *sail* to help give it shape. They vary in length depending on the sail design.
• **Beam reach** *Point of sailing* when the wind is blowing at 90 degrees to the *centerline* of the *board*.
• **Bear away** To turn the front of the *board* away from the wind.
• **Beaufort scale** System used to relate wind strength to physical effects.
• **Board** Buoyant platform supporting the sailor and *rig*.
• **Boom** Wishbone-shaped assembly which is used to support the *sail* and control the *rig*.
• **Bow** The front of the *board*.
• **Broad reach** The *point of sailing* when the wind blows approximately 90 to 160 degrees to the *centerline*.
• **Buoyancy aid** A jacket that aids flotation in the water.

C

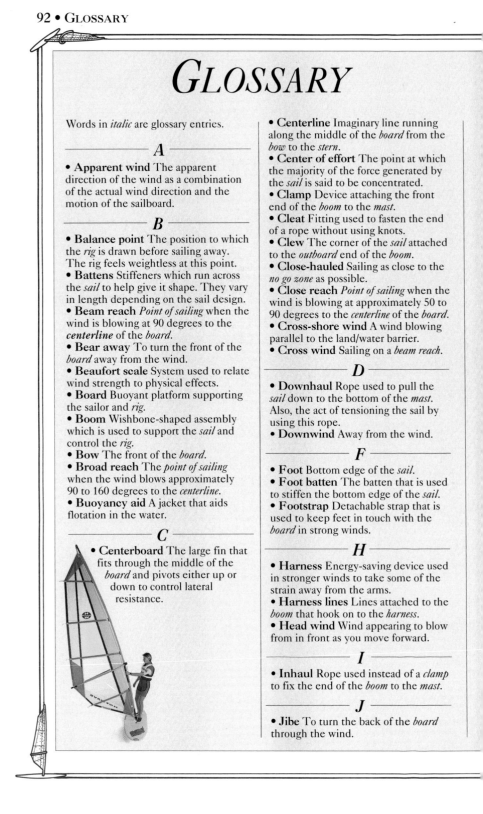

• **Centerboard** The large fin that fits through the middle of the *board* and pivots either up or down to control lateral resistance.

• **Centerline** Imaginary line running along the middle of the *board* from the *bow* to the *stern*.
• **Center of effort** The point at which the majority of the force generated by the *sail* is said to be concentrated.
• **Clamp** Device attaching the front end of the *boom* to the *mast*.
• **Cleat** Fitting used to fasten the end of a rope without using knots.
• **Clew** The corner of the *sail* attached to the *outboard* end of the *boom*.
• **Close-hauled** Sailing as close to the *no go zone* as possible.
• **Close reach** *Point of sailing* when the wind is blowing at approximately 50 to 90 degrees to the *centerline* of the *board*.
• **Cross-shore wind** A wind blowing parallel to the land/water barrier.
• **Cross wind** Sailing on a *beam reach*.

D

• **Downhaul** Rope used to pull the *sail* down to the bottom of the *mast*. Also, the act of tensioning the sail by using this rope.
• **Downwind** Away from the wind.

F

• **Foot** Bottom edge of the *sail*.
• **Foot batten** The batten that is used to stiffen the bottom edge of the *sail*.
• **Footstrap** Detachable strap that is used to keep feet in touch with the *board* in strong winds.

H

• **Harness** Energy-saving device used in stronger winds to take some of the strain away from the arms.
• **Harness lines** Lines attached to the *boom* that hook on to the *harness*.
• **Head wind** Wind appearing to blow from in front as you move forward.

I

• **Inhaul** Rope used instead of a *clamp* to fix the end of the *boom* to the *mast*.

J

• **Jibe** To turn the back of the *board* through the wind.

L

• **Leech** The back edge of the *sail*.
• **Leeward** On or towards the side turned away from the wind.
• **Luff** To turn the front of the *board* away from the wind; the front edge of the *sail* comprising the *mast sleeve*.
• **Luff tube** The sleeve on the front of the *sail* into which the *mast* slides (same as *mast sleeve*).

M

• **Mast** Main spar which supports the front edge of the *sail*.
• **Mast foot** Assembly at the bottom of the *mast* attaching the *rig* to the *board* which includes the *universal joint* which is so critical to the sailboard design.
• **Mast sleeve** Same as *Luff tube*
• **Mast track** Adjustable track on the top of the *board* which carries the *mast foot* assembly.

N

• **No go zone** An area approximately 50 degrees on either side of the wind into which the *board* cannot possibly be sailed as all power is lost.

O

• **Offshore wind** A wind blowing off the land and onto the water.
• **Onshore wind** A wind blowing off the water and onto the land.
• **Outboard** Positioned away from the *centerline* of the sailboard.
• **Outhaul** Rope used to attach the *sail* to the *outboard* end of the *boom*. The act of tensioning the sail horizontally using the outhaul rope.

P

• **Pivot point** A point on the *board* around which it turns. It changes in relation to a number of variables, such as the wind strength and the position of the sailor on the board.
• **Points of sailing** The various directions in which the *board* can possibly be sailed.
• **Port** The left side of the *board* when facing towards the *bow*.

R

• **Reaching** Fast *point of sailing* when traveling across the wind.

• **Rig** Assembly consisting of the *sail*, *mast*, *mast foot*, and *boom*.
• **Running** *Point of sailing* when the wind is blowing from directly behind the sailboard.

S

• **Safety leash** Rope or strap retaining the *rig* if the *mast foot* becomes separated.
• **Sail** Material extended on rigging which propels the *board* by offering resistance to the wind.
• **Sheet in** To pull in the *sail* with the back hand on the *boom* in order to increase the power.
• **Sheet out** Ease out the *sail* with the back hand to reduce power.
• **Skeg** The small fin attached to the underside of the *board* which gives it directional stability.
• **Starboard** The right-hand side of the *board* when facing the *bow*.
• **Stern** The back of the *board*.

T

• **Tack** Turn the front of the *board* through the wind.
• **Towing eye** The eye at the front or the back of the *board* to which a rope can be attached.
• **Trimming** Adjusting the *sail* to suit the prevailing wind.

U

• **Universal joint** Flexible connection allowing the *rig* to pivot in any direction.
• **Uphaul** Thick rope used to pull the *sail* up out of the water.
• **Upwind** Towards the wind.

W

• **Windward** The side towards the wind.

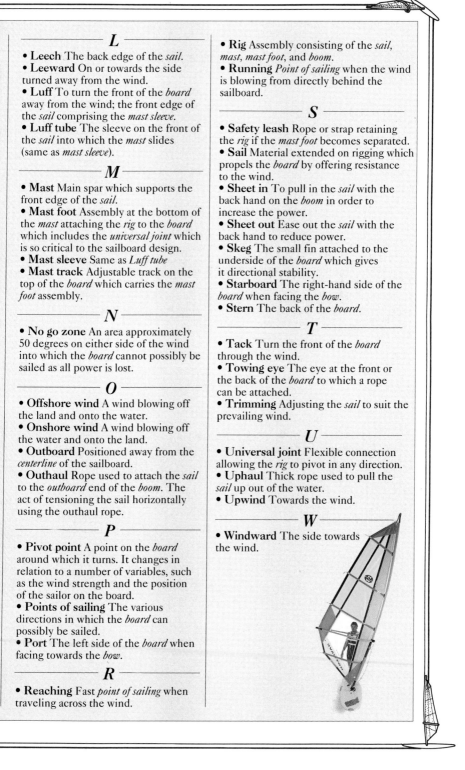

INDEX

GETTING IN TOUCH

U.S. Windsurfing Assoc.	Professional Boardsailers	Windsurfing Magazine
Box 978	Association	P.O. Box 8500
Hood River, Oregon	61 London Road	Winter Park, Florida
97031	Datchet, Slough	32790-9825
503-386-8708	SL3 9JY England	(for subscriptions)

ACKNOWLEDGMENTS

Phil Jones and Dorling Kindersley would like to thank the following for their
contribution and support in the production of this book:

Suzy Hornby and John Manners for their modelling and expertise.
David Thomas of Club Sportif, Suite 1225, The Gatwick Hilton Hotel, Gatwick,
West Sussex, RH6 OLL, (tel. 0293 567396), for flights and accomodation in
Lanzarote for location photography.
Scanro for the loan of Vinta boards, Unit 99/15 North Tyne Industrial Estate,
Longbenton, Newcastle upon Tyne, Tyne and Wear, NE 9SZ, (tel. 091 226 9222).
Kenneth Gasque at Club la Santa, Lanzarote, for use of their excellent facilities.
The London Dinghy Centre, 232 Hither Green Lane, London SE13 6RT, for the
loan of windsurfing equipment.
Windsurfers World Ltd, 146 Chiswick Green High Rd, London W4 1PU, for the
loan of windsurfing clothes and accessories.
Hilary Bird for preparing the index.
Rodney Forte and Tracy Hambleton for coping with carnets.
Ann Kay, Jo Weeks, Debz Opoczynska, and Lol Henderson for editorial assistance.
Rodney Forte for photographic assistance.
4 Walls Studios, 5 Defoe Rd, Stoke Newington, London, N12, for studio hire.
John Woodcock for the full-colour illustrations.
Coral Mula, John Woodcock, Janos Marffy,
Rob Shone, Salvo Tomaselli, and Nicholas
Hall for black and white line illustrations.